Nomographs for Estimating Surface Fire Behavior Characteristics

Joe H. Scott

United States
Department
of Agriculture

Forest Service

Rocky Mountain
Research Station

General Technical
Report RMRS-GTR-192

May 2007

CORRECTIONS FOR

RMRS GTR-192

Nomographs for estimating surface fire behavior characteristics

A pervasive mislabeling has been discovered in the wind vectoring charts within RMRS-GTR-192. The label for the wind direction 315 degrees clockwise from upslope (upper-left quadrant of the chart; 45 degrees anticlockwise) is erroneously labeled "305". This error occurs on every wind vectoring chart in the report, including the examples. The correct label should be "315", as shown below.

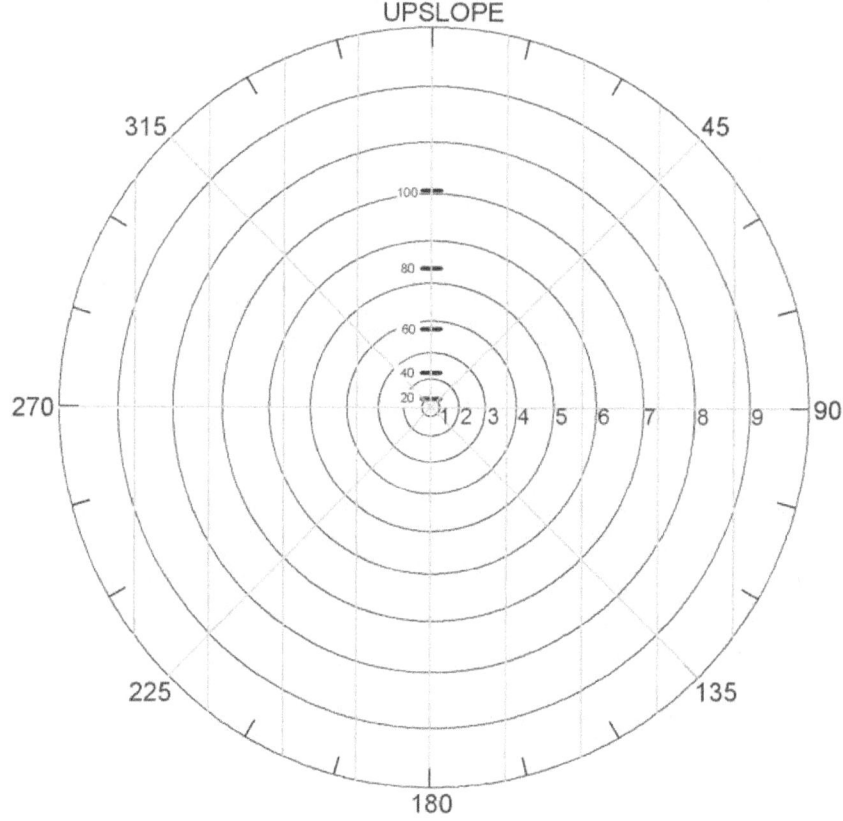

The labels have been corrected in the electronic format of the GTR, as well as in the PDF files available at the website of the Fire Modeling Institute (www.fs.fed.us/fmi).

Scott, Joe H. 2007. **Nomographs for estimating surface fire behavior characteristics**. Gen. Tech. Rep. RMRS-GTR-192. Fort Collins, CO: U.S. Department of Agriculture, Forest Service, Rocky Mountain Research Station. 119 p.

Abstract

A complete set of nomographs for estimating surface fire rate of spread and flame length for the original 13 and new 40 fire behavior fuel models is presented. The nomographs allow calculation of spread rate and flame length for wind in any direction with respect to slope and allow for non-heading spread directions. Basic instructions for use are included.

Keywords: rate of spread, flame length, fire behavior prediction, fuel model

The Author

Joe H. Scott is a Research Forester with Systems for Environmental Management in Missoula, Montana. Joe earned a B.S. in Forestry and Resource Management from the University of California at Berkeley, and an M.S. in Forestry from the University of Montana. He is a Certified Forester™ as recognized by the Society of American Foresters.

Acknowledgments

I thank Don Carlton, Fire Program Solutions, for suggesting the simplified nomograph format; Cassie Koerner and Violet Holley, Missoula Fire Sciences Lab, for formatting and error-checking the charts; and Bret Butler and Dan Jimenez, Missoula Fire Sciences Lab, and Laurie Kurth, Fire Modeling Institute, for reviewing the draft manuscript. Funding for preparation and publication of the nomographs was provided by the U.S. Forest Service Washington Office fire technology transfer program, and by the Fire Modeling Institute, Missoula Fire Sciences Lab, Rocky Mountain Research Station, U.S. Forest Service. Brad Reed coined the term "hanking" fire behavior (referring to fire behavior between the head and flank of the fire).

Contents

Nomographs for Estimating Surface Fire Behavior Characteristics

Joe H. Scott

Introduction

A nomograph is a visual representation of numerical relationships. Nomographs are useful for graphically illustrating sensitivity of a model to its inputs, as well as for estimating model outputs without a computer. Albini (1976) produced a set of nomographs for estimating wildland fire behavior characteristics for the original 13 fire behavior fuel models (Albini 1976, Anderson 1982) based on Rothermel's (1972) surface fire spread model. Albini's nomographs calculated fire characteristics in the heading direction only. The effect of wind speed could only be calculated in the upslope direction.

Andrews (1986) produced a computer program for estimating wildland fire behavior—the BEHAVE fire behavior modeling system. At this time, computers were not readily available to Fire Behavior Officers while on fire assignments or for fire behavior training courses, so the nomographs continued to receive frequent use even after the advent of BEHAVE. Today, Fire Behavior Analysts still use Albini's nomographs for making simple fire behavior predictions when a computer is not available. An additional set of 40 standard fire behavior fuel models was recently made available (Scott and Burgan 2005). Many Fire Behavior Analysts requested that nomographs be created for those fuel models.

There are three significant changes in format and operation with these new nomographs. First, the limitation to upslope wind direction has been eliminated with the development of a separate chart for combining the effects of wind speed, wind direction, and slope steepness. Second, the limitation to computing fire behavior in the heading direction only has been eliminated with the development of a separate chart for reducing head fire spread rate and flame length to appropriate values for non-heading spread directions. Finally, the nomographs have been reformatted to focus on primary model inputs (fuel moisture and effective midflame wind speed) and primary outputs (rate of spread and flame length). The original format allowed the user to compute intermediate model results (reaction intensity and propagating flux). The new format estimates outputs directly, without showing intermediate results. For sake of completeness, nomographs for the original 13 fuel models have been created in the new format.

Gathering Inputs

Gathering the required inputs is the first step in using the nomographs (Procedures for selecting a fuel model and estimating other input values are covered in training courses and other reports.). Inputs are required in the following categories: fuel and moisture, wind and slope, and spread direction. All inputs and outputs can be recorded on the nomograph worksheet provided in this report (p. 14).

Fuel and Moisture Inputs—The first fuel input to specify is the fuel model. Any of the original 13 or new 40 fire behavior fuel models may be selected.

Dead fuel moisture content is a required input for all fuel models. To be consistent with predictions made with computerized fire behavior prediction systems, the dead fuel moisture content input should be the surface-area-weighted average moisture content of the 1-, 10-, and 100-h timelag classes (Rothermel 1972). Weighting factors vary by fuel model, but in all cases are weighted heavily toward the 1-h timelag class (table 1). Therefore, the moisture content of the 1-h timelag class can be used for the dead fuel moisture input without significant error. For more precision, or to match the results from computerized applications, compute the weighted-average dead fuel moisture using the weighting factors listed in table 1.

Live herbaceous (LHMC) and live woody moisture content (LWMC) inputs are required only if the selected fuel model contains fuel in one of those components (see table 1). LHMC has a strong effect on predicted fire behavior in the new fuel model set (Jolly 2005)

USDA Forest Service Gen. Tech. Rep. RMRS-GTR-192. 2007

1

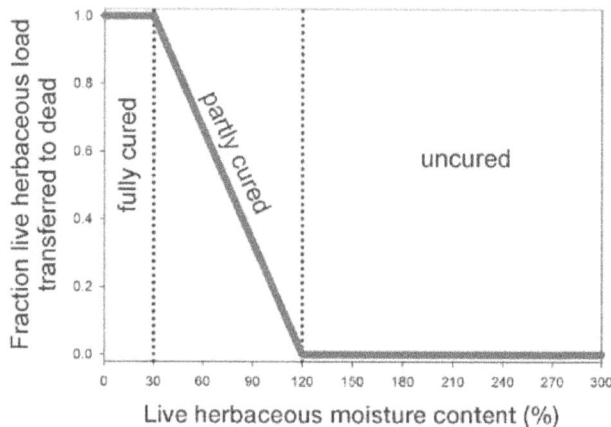

Table 1—Weighting factors for calculating weighted-average dead fuel moisture content, presence of live fuel component, and wind adjustment factor (WAF) for the original 13 and new 40 fire behavior fuel models. Weighting factors assume all herbaceous load is in the 1-h class (full curing). WAF values were estimated using Albini and Baughman's (1979) model of wind reduction over exposed fuelbeds on flat terrain assuming flame height is twice fuelbed depth. Values in this table match those used in BehavePlus, FARSITE, and FlamMap.

Fuel model	Weighting factors			Live fuel		WAF
	1-h	10-h	100-h	Herb	Woody	
1	1.00	0.00	0.00			0.36
2	0.98	0.02	0.00	√		0.36
3	1.00	0.00	0.00			0.44
4	0.95	0.04	0.01		√	0.55
5	0.97	0.03	0.00		√	0.42
6	0.89	0.09	0.02			0.44
7	0.89	0.09	0.02		√	0.44
8	0.94	0.03	0.02			0.28
9	0.99	0.01	0.00			0.28
10	0.94	0.03	0.02		√	0.36
11	0.77	0.17	0.06			0.36
12	0.75	0.19	0.06			0.43
13	0.76	0.18	0.06			0.46
GR1	1.00	0.00	0.00	√		0.31
GR2	1.00	0.00	0.00	√		0.36
GR3	0.98	0.02	0.00	√		0.42
GR4	1.00	0.00	0.00	√		0.42
GR5	1.00	0.00	0.00	√		0.39
GR6	1.00	0.00	0.00	√		0.39
GR7	1.00	0.00	0.00	√		0.46
GR8	0.99	0.01	0.00	√		0.49
GR9	0.99	0.01	0.00	√		0.52
GS1	1.00	0.00	0.00	√	√	0.35
GS2	0.97	0.03	0.00	√	√	0.39
GS3	0.99	0.01	0.00	√	√	0.41
GS4	1.00	0.00	0.00	√	√	0.42
SH1	0.97	0.03	0.00	√	√	0.36
SH2	0.90	0.09	0.01		√	0.36
SH3	0.69	0.31	0.00		√	0.44
SH4	0.93	0.07	0.00		√	0.46
SH5	0.92	0.08	0.00		√	0.55
SH6	0.93	0.07	0.00		√	0.42
SH7	0.80	0.18	0.02		√	0.55
SH8	0.80	0.19	0.01		√	0.46
SH9	0.96	0.04	0.00	√	√	0.50
TU1	0.84	0.11	0.05	√	√	0.33
TU2	0.89	0.09	0.02		√	0.36
TU3	0.99	0.01	0.00	√	√	0.38
TU4	1.00	0.00	0.00		√	0.32
TU5	0.92	0.07	0.01		√	0.36
TL1	0.85	0.10	0.05			0.28
TL2	0.90	0.08	0.02			0.28
TL3	0.76	0.18	0.06			0.29
TL4	0.78	0.13	0.10			0.31
TL5	0.85	0.10	0.05			0.33
TL6	0.97	0.03	0.01			0.29
TL7	0.60	0.15	0.24			0.31
TL8	0.98	0.01	0.00			0.29
TL9	0.96	0.03	0.01			0.33
SB1	0.82	0.09	0.09			0.36
SB2	0.94	0.05	0.01			0.36
SB3	0.97	0.03	0.01			0.38
SB4	0.95	0.03	0.01			0.45

because dynamic load transfer is tied to LHMC (Scott and Burgan 2005). Dynamic load transfer is the simulation of curing in herbaceous fuels by shifting herbaceous fuel load from the live component to dead where it takes on the moisture content of the 1-h timelag class. The transfer of live herbaceous load to dead is a function of LHMC (Burgan 1979), on the assumption that LHMC decreases as curing takes place. For LHMC ≥ 120 percent, no herbaceous load is transferred to dead; all herbaceous fuel is green and at the specified LHMC, and fire behavior is correspondingly benign. For LHMC ≤ 30 percent, all herbaceous load is transferred to dead; none remains in the live component, and fire behavior is at its maximum potential for the fuel model. For LHMC between 30 and 120 percent, a fraction of the load is transferred to dead (fig. 1). The degree of curing is therefore an important factor for determining a LHMC value (see table 2).

Wind and Slope Inputs—Slope steepness for the nomographs is measured in percent. Estimating slope to the nearest 10 percent is sufficient.

An estimate of midflame wind speed is required, and can be estimated by direct observation or by multiplying 20-ft wind speed by a wind adjustment factor (WAF). On flat terrain, WAF can be determined using tables based on Albini and Baughman's (1979) models of wind reduction. Those same models are used in BehavePlus, FARSITE, and FlamMap. If the surface fuelbed in question is sheltered by a forest canopy (canopy cover greater than 5 percent), use table 3, otherwise, use table 1.

Figure 1—Transfer of live herbaceous load to dead herbaceous load as a function of live herbaceous moisture content (LHMC). If necessary, use the observed degree of curing (fraction of load transfer) of the herbaceous fuels to determine a value for LHMC.

2

USDA Forest Service Gen. Tech. Rep. RMRS-GTR-192. 2007

Table 2—Live herbaceous moisture content (LHMC) values to use for various degrees of curing. LHMC in the nomographs is linked to degree of curing, meaning herbaceous fuel is transferred from live to dead as a function of LHMC.

Degree of curing	LHMC (percent)
Fully cured	30
Two-thirds cured	60
One-half cured	75
One-third cured	90
Uncured (fully green)	120

Wind direction for the nomographs is the direction the wind is pushing the fire, and is entered in degrees clockwise from upslope. For example, a cross-slope wind blowing from left to right (while facing upslope) is pushing the fire in the direction 90 degrees clockwise from upslope.

Spread Direction—Basic nomograph outputs are rate of spread and flame length in the direction of maximum spread—the heading direction. By assuming fire spreads as a simple ellipse, spread rate and flame length can also be estimated in other spread directions (see Appendix A). Flanking fire behavior occurs at the widest part of the ellipse where the flame front is

Table 3—Wind adjustment factor (WAF) for surface fuel sheltered by a forest canopy (canopy cover greater than 5 percent), as a function of canopy cover (CC). WAF values were stylized for this table based on output from Albini and Baughman's (1979) model of wind reduction by a forest canopy. See table 1 for WAF values to use for unsheltered fuelbeds.

Canopy cover (percent)	WAF
CC ≤ 5	use table 1
5 < CC ≤ 10	0.30
10 < CC ≤ 15	0.25
15 < CC ≤ 30	0.20
30 < CC ≤ 50	0.15
CC > 50	0.10

oriented perpendicular to the heading direction, while backing fire behavior occurs at the rear (directly opposite the heading direction). The chart also allows calculation of "hanking" fire behavior—fire behavior between the head and flank of a fire—where the flame front is oriented 45 degrees off the heading direction (fig. 2).

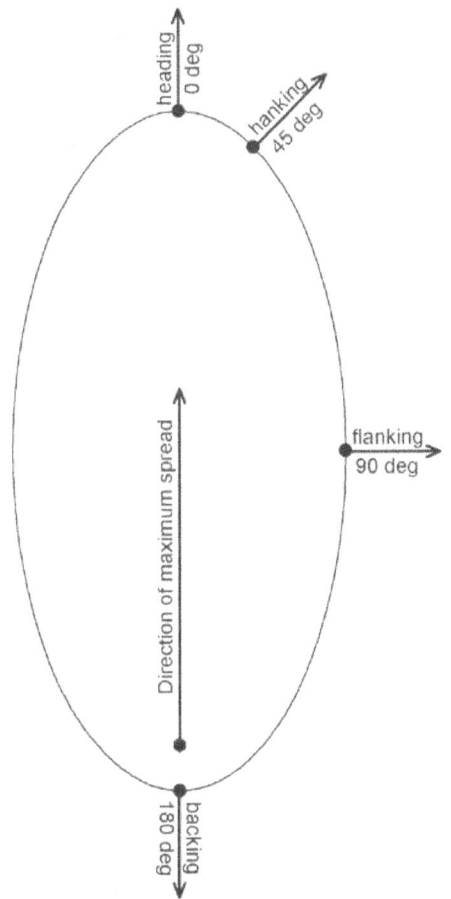

Figure 2—Locations of heading, hanking, flanking, and backing spread calculations around an elliptical fire. Heading fire calculations are made for the direction of maximum spread. Flanking fire calculations are made for the widest part of the ellipse, where the fire front is oriented perpendicular to the maximum spread direction. Backing fire calculations are made for the rear of the fire, directly opposite the maximum spread direction. Hanking fire calculations are made for the point on the perimeter where the flame front is oriented 45 degrees away from the maximum spread direction (The term "hanking" refers to fire behavior between the head and flank of a fire.).

Estimating Fire Behavior With Nomographs

Once the inputs are gathered, estimating fire behavior with nomographs is a three-step process. The first step is to estimate effective midflame wind speed using the wind vectoring chart provided with each nomograph. The next step is to estimate rate of spread and flame length in the direction of maximum spread. For this step, nomograph format and use depends on whether the selected fuel model contains a live fuel component (either herbaceous or woody). In the new fuel model set, only the timber litter (TL) and slash/blowdown (SB) fuel models do not have a live fuel component; the grass (GR), grass-shrub (GS), shrub (SH), and timber-understory (TU) fuel models contain herbaceous and/or woody fuel. Original fuel models 2, 4, 5, 7, and 10 contain live fuel; 1, 3, 6, 8, 9, and 11 through 13 do not. The final step, if necessary, is to estimate rate of spread and flame length in a non-heading direction. This is accomplished with a single chart applicable to all fuel models. These three steps are described separately in the following sections.

Step 1: Effective Midflame Wind Speed

The procedure for estimating effective midflame wind speed is the same for all fuel models, but there is a unique pair of wind vectoring charts for each fuel model, one for low wind speeds and another for high. If you are not certain whether the effective wind speed will be low or high, start with the chart for low wind speeds and switch to the higher one if necessary. For fuel models without a live fuel component, both vectoring charts are on the same page. For fuel models with a live herbaceous or live woody fuel component, the vectoring charts are on separate pages.

Estimation of midflame wind speed will be demonstrated with the following example: fuel model TL5, slope steepness 60 percent, midflame wind speed 7 mi/h, and wind direction 135 degrees clockwise from uphill. Inputs and results for this and following examples are shown in a nomograph worksheet (fig. 3).

1) Select the nomograph and wind vectoring chart.

Select the nomograph for TL5, and then locate the vectoring chart for low wind speeds (the upper "bullseye" chart on the nomograph page).

2) Determine the effective midflame wind speed.
   a. Draw a vertical line from the origin of the concentric circles to the point on the line corresponding to the slope steepness. Interpolate between tick marks as necessary (fig. 4, line a). This line represents the slope vector (direction and magnitude of the effect of slope on fire spread).
   b. Draw a line from the origin of the concentric circles in the direction the wind is pushing the fire. Stop the line at the circle representing the midflame wind speed (fig. 4, line b). Each circle represents 1 mi/h wind speed (2 mi/h for high wind speed nomographs). Interpolate between circles as necessary. Faint gray diagonal and horizontal lines aid in drawing lines along common wind directions: quarter up-slope, cross-slope, and quarter down-slope. Tick marks around the perimeter of the chart indicate 15 degree increments of wind direction. The line you have just drawn represents the wind vector (direction and magnitude of the effect of wind on fire spread).
   c. Draw a vertical line from the end of the wind vector (fig. 4, line c). Use the vertical gray lines on the chart to assist in drawing the line.
   d. Draw a line parallel to the wind vector, beginning from the tip of the slope vector and continuing to (or beyond) the vertical line drawn in line c above (fig. 4, line d).
   e. Draw a line from the origin to the intersection of lines c and d. This line is the effective wind vector (fig. 4, line e).
   f. The direction of the effective wind vector indicates the direction of maximum fire spread. Trace this line to the outer circle, and then read the direction to within 5 degrees clockwise from upslope. For this example, the result is 110 degrees clockwise from upslope (fig. 4, point f).
   g. The length of the effective wind vector indicates the effective midflame wind speed. Read that value by interpolating between circles. For this example, the result is 5.8 mi/h (see fig. 4).

Fire Behavior Nomograph Worksheet

		\			
analyst name:	*Joe Scott*				
project name:	**Nomograph examples**				
projection date and time:					

notes:		**Projection Point**			notes:
		A	B	C	

Fuel and Moisture

		A	B		
(1)	Fuel model	TL5	SH5		category
(2)	dead woody fuel moisture	5	5		percent
(3)	live herbaceous fuel moisture	- -	- -		percent
(4)	live woody fuel moisture	- -	110		percent

Wind and Slope

		A	B		
(5)	slope steepness	60	60		percent
(6)	Canopy cover	- -	0		percent
(7)	20-ft wind speed	- -	10		mi/h
(8)	Wind Adjustment Factor	- -	0.5		fraction (table 3 or 4)
(9)	midflame wind speed	7	5		mi/h (direct entry or [7] x [8])
(10)	wind direction	135	90		degrees clockwise from upslope

Spread Direction

		A	B		
(11)	spread direction	**head**	**flank**		(heading, hanking, flanking, or backing)

Results

		A	B		
(12)	effective midflame wind speed	5.8	5.5		mi/h
(13)	direction of maximum spread	110	64		degrees clockwise from upslope
(14)	head fire rate of spread	6	56		ch/h
(15)	head fire flame length	2.5	13.5		ft
(16)	length-to-breadth ratio	- -	2.4		ratio
(17)	fraction of head fire rate of spread	- -	0.22		fraction
(18)	fraction of head fire flame length	- -	0.50		fraction
(19)	rate of spread in spread direction	6	12		ch/h ([14] x [17])
(20)	flame length in spread direction	2.5	6.8		ft ([15] x [18])

Figure 3—Example Fire Behavior Nomograph Worksheet for recording inputs and outputs for the examples in the text. See text for complete instructions.

Step 2: Head Fire Rate of Spread and Flame Length

The procedure for estimating head fire rate of spread and flame length depends on whether the selected fuel model contains a live fuel component. For fuel models without live fuel, nomographs for low and high wind speeds are printed on the same page, and the only inputs needed are effective midflame wind speed (from previous step) and dead fuel moisture content. For fuel models with a live fuel component, charts for low wind speeds and high wind speeds are on separate pages. An additional input, live fuel moisture content, is required to use these charts. The different procedures for using these nomographs are presented in the following sections.

Fuel Models Without a Live Component—The use of a nomograph to estimate fire behavior in the heading direction for a fuel model without a live fuel component will be illustrated by continuing the previous example: Fuel model TL5; slope steepness 60 percent; midflame wind speed 7 mi/h; and wind direction 135 degrees clockwise from upslope (quarter-downslope). Resulting effective midflame wind speed was 5.8 mi/h. Additionally, we will use a dead fuel moisture content of 5 percent. Inputs and outputs for this example are displayed on a Fire Behavior Nomograph Worksheet (fig. 3, Projection Point A).

1) Determine head fire rate of spread and flame length.
   a. Draw a vertical line beginning from the bottom axis of the chart at a value corresponding to the dead fuel moisture content—5 percent in this example (fig. 4, line g).

USDA Forest Service Gen. Tech. Rep. RMRS-GTR-192. 2007

5

TL5 (185)

low wind speeds

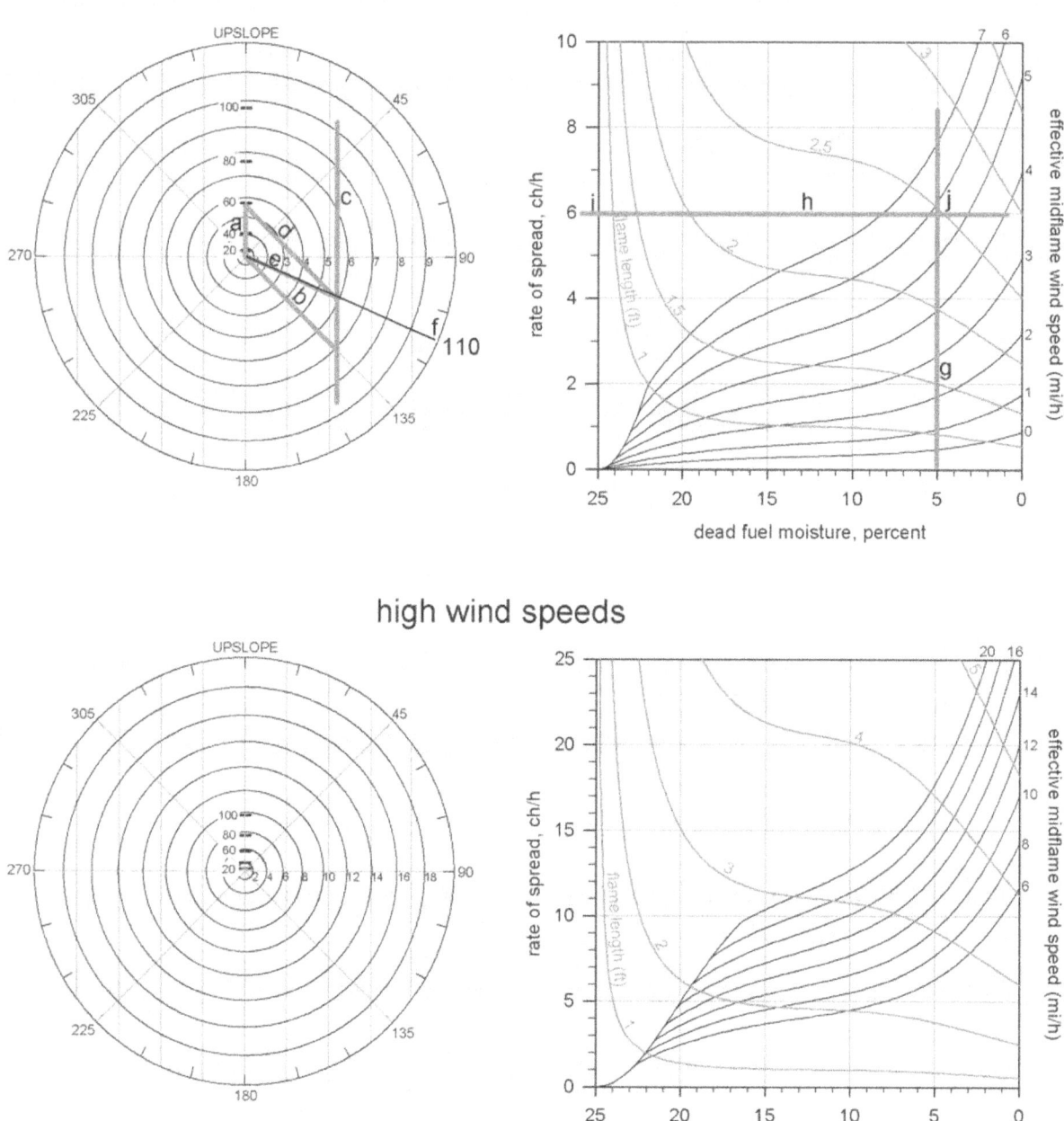

high wind speeds

Figure 4—Example nomograph for estimating effective midflame wind speed and head fire rate of spread and flame length for fuel model TL5. Inputs: slope steepness = 60 percent; midflame wind speed = 7 mi/h; wind direction = 135 degrees clockwise from uphill; and dead fuel moisture content = 5 percent. Results: effective midflame wind speed = 5.8 mi/h; direction of maximum spread = 110 degrees; head fire rate of spread = 6 ch/h; and head fire flame length = 2.5 feet. Annotations refer to instructions in text.

b. Mark the point where this vertical line crosses the line for the effective midflame wind speed determined in the previous example (5.8 mi/h). If necessary, interpolate between lines for effective midflame wind speed. The lines are labeled at the right-hand axis. For example, place the mark 80 percent of the way between the lines for 5 and 6 mi/h effective midflame wind speeds. Draw a horizontal line from this point to the left-hand axis. Use the faint gray lines as a guide (fig. 4, line h).

c. Read the head fire rate of spread (ch/h) from the left-hand axis (fig. 4, point i). The result for this example is 6 ch/h.

d. Read the head fire flame length (feet) by interpolating between the curving gray lines representing flame length (fig. 4, point j). The result for this example is 2.5 ft.

Fuel Models With a Live Component—The following example inputs will be used to illustrate the use of a nomograph to estimate head fire behavior for a fuel model with a live fuel component: Fuel model SH5; slope steepness 60 percent; no canopy cover; 20-ft wind speed 7 mi/h; upslope wind direction; live woody moisture content 110 percent; and dead fuel moisture content 5 percent. Input and outputs are recorded on a Fire Behavior Nomograph Worksheet (fig. 3, Projection Point B). For this example we will repeat the first step, vectoring wind and slope, to illustrate the process for the upslope wind direction.

1) Select the nomograph and wind vectoring chart.

Select the nomograph for SH5, low wind speeds.

2) Determine the effective midflame wind speed.

We first need to determine midflame wind speed from the 20-ft wind speed. Because there is no canopy cover, WAF is determined from table 1. For SH5, WAF is 0.55. Therefore, midflame wind speed is 7 x 0.55, or 3.9 mi/h. Manual vectoring of wind and slope effects is most difficult with wind blowing directly upslope or downslope, as it is in this example.

a. Draw a vertical line from the origin of the concentric circles to the point on the line corresponding to the slope steepness. Interpolate between tick marks as necessary (fig. 5, line a).

b. Draw another vertical line from the origin of the concentric circles to the circle representing the midflame wind speed. To avoid overlapping the line drawn in 2a, you may need to offset this line slightly (fig. 5, line b).

c. Now, draw a clone of line a (same length) beginning at the upper end of line b (fig. 5, line c).

d. Read the effective midflame wind speed by noting where the tip of line c falls (fig. 5, point d). In this example, the effective midflame wind speed is 5.9 mi/h. With upslope winds, direction of maximum spread is always upslope.

3) Select a specific chart on the page.

The nomograph pages for fuel models with live fuel consist of five separate charts, each for a different live fuel moisture content. For fuel models with both herbaceous and woody live fuel load, live fuel moisture refers to the live herbaceous moisture content. Live woody moisture content is assumed to be 30 percent higher than live herbaceous fuel. Select the chart matching the live moisture content value and follow steps a through d for the "no live fuel" nomographs to determine spread rate and flame length. If you need to determine spread rate or flame length for a live moisture content value between the values for which a chart is available, make the calculations using the two charts that bracket the value and interpolate. The following example illustrates the interpolation process.

4) Determine the head fire rate of spread and flame length.

a. Draw a vertical line from the bottom of the nomograph corresponding to the specified dead fuel moisture content. In this example, we need to interpolate between two nomographs, so draw this vertical line on the two charts that bracket the desired LWMC (fig. 5, lines e).

b. On both charts, mark the point where this vertical line crosses the line for the effective midflame wind speed estimated above (5.9 mi/h in this example). If necessary, interpolate between lines (labeled at the right-hand axes) for effective midflame wind speed. Draw horizontal lines from these points to the common y-axis. Use the faint gray lines as a guide. Do this for both charts (fig. 5, lines f).

c. Read the rate of spread (ch/h) for both charts and then interpolate between them. In this example, rate of spread for 100 percent LWMC is about 66 ch/h, and for 120 percent LWMC is about 56 ch/h. Therefore, rate of spread for 110 percent LWMC would be about halfway between those two estimates, or 61 ch/h (fig. 5, point g).

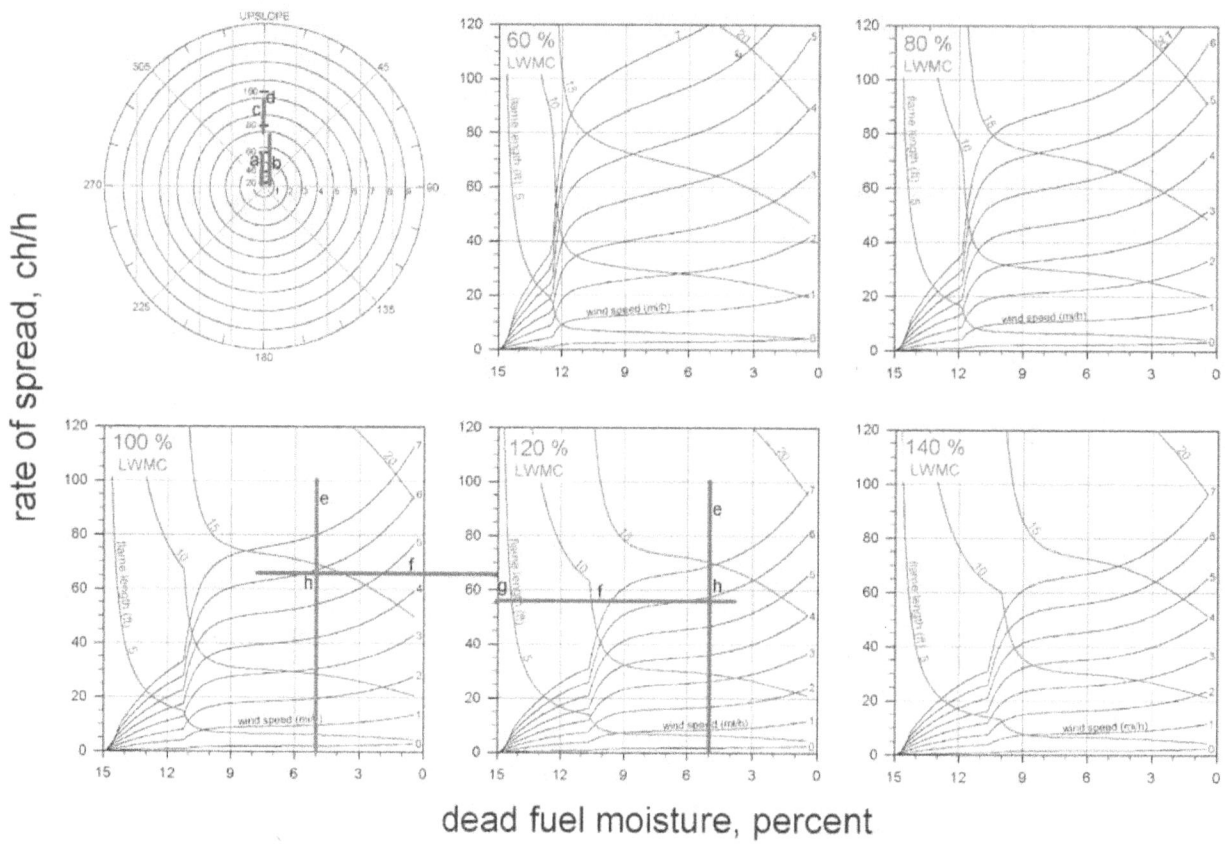

Figure 5—Example nomograph for estimating effective midflame wind speed and head fire rate of spread and flame length for fuel model SH5. Inputs: slope steepness = 60 percent; midflame wind speed 3.9 = mi/h; wind direction = upslope; dead fuel moisture content 5 percent; and live woody fuel moisture content = 110 percent. Results: effective midflame wind speed = 5.9 mi/h; head fire rate of spread = 61 ch/h; and head fire flame length = 14 feet. Annotations refer to instructions in the text.

d. Read the flame length for each chart separately by interpolating between the curving gray lines representing flame length. The separate flame length estimates are about 14.5 ft for 100 percent LWMC and about 13.5 ft for 120 percent LWMC; the resulting interpolation for 110 percent LWMC is therefore 14 ft (fig. 5, points h).

Step 3: Non-heading Rate of Spread and Flame Length

We determined potential head fire rate of spread and flame length in previous examples. In this section we will demonstrate how to adjust those predictions for

other parts of an elliptical fire using the "Fire Behavior in Non-heading Directions Nomograph" (p. 13). The equations used for estimating non-heading rate of spread and flame length are documented in Appendix A. For this example, we will use the results from the example (fuel models with a live component) to estimate rate of spread and flame length at the flank of the fire. In that example, effective midflame wind speed was 5.9 mi/h; head fire rate of spread was 61 ch/h; and head fire flame length was 14 ft.

a. Beginning with the right-hand chart of the nomograph, draw a vertical line from the bottom axis to the top at the effective midflame wind speed (fig. 6, line a).

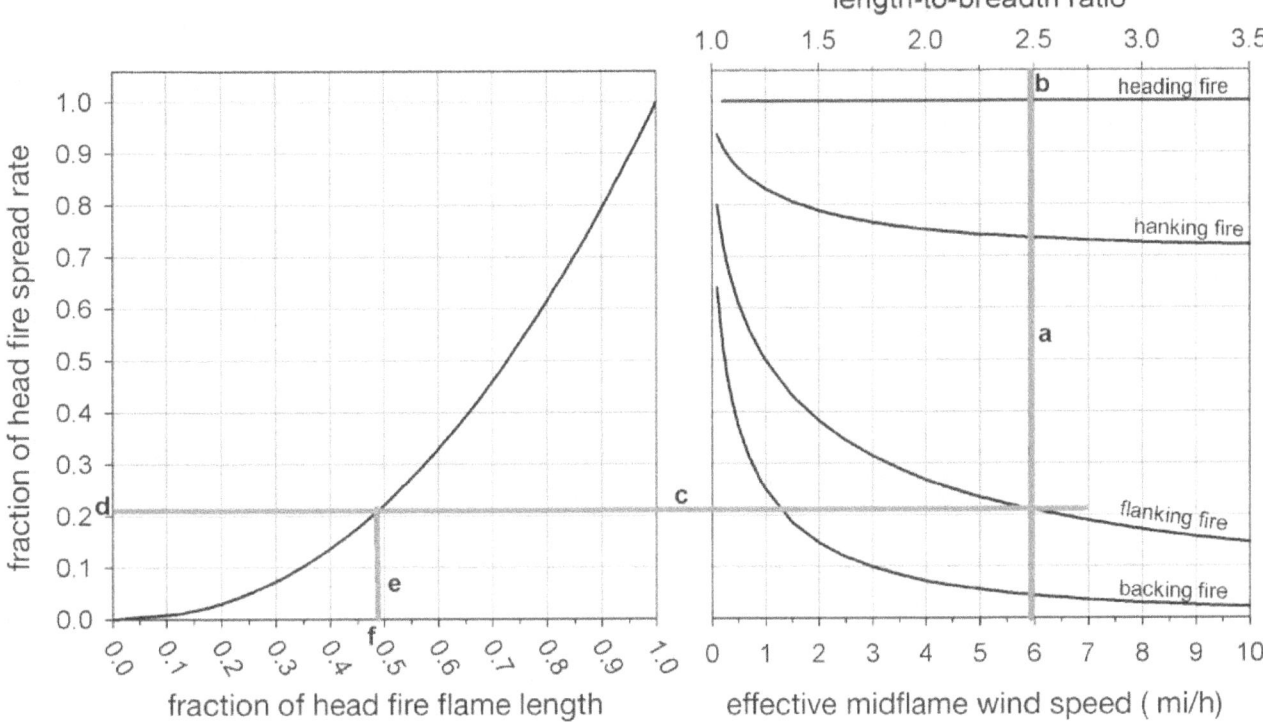

Figure 6—Example nomograph for estimating rate of spread and flame length in non-heading directions. Annotations refer to instructions in text. Inputs: effective midflame wind speed = 5.9 mi/h (see fig. 5); spread direction = flanking fire; head fire rate of spread = 61 ch/h (see fig. 5); and head fire flame length = 14 ft (see fig. 5). Results: length-to-breadth ratio = 2.5; fraction of head fire rate of spread = 0.21; rate of spread in flanking direction = 13 ch/h; fraction of head fire flame length = 0.49; and flame length at flank of fire = 7 ft.

b. Read the corresponding value for length-to-breadth ratio from the top axis. The length-to-breadth ratio for this example is 2.5 (fig. 6, point b). This value will be useful in plotting a point-source fire on a map.

c. Next, draw a horizontal line from the intersection of the vertical line drawn in step 5a and the line corresponding to the desired spread direction. Ensure the line goes all the way to the left-axis of the left-hand chart (fig. 6, line c).

d. Read the resulting fraction of head fire rate of spread from the left-axis of the left-hand chart. Multiply the head fire rate of spread by this fraction (0.21 in this example) to estimate flanking spread rate. The result for this example is 13 ch/h (figure 6, point d).

e. Draw a vertical line from the intersection of line 5c and the curving line in the left-hand chart to the bottom axis (fig. 6, line e).

f. Read the resulting fraction of head fire flame length from the bottom axis. Multiply the head fire flame length by this fraction (0.49 in this example) to estimate flame length in the chosen spread direction. The result for this example is 7 ft (fig. 6, point f).

Summary

Nomographs are useful for estimating surface fire behavior characteristics in situations where a computer is not available and for visually depicting the relationships among input and output variables. The recent development of 40 standard fire behavior fuel models required that additional nomographs be created. A more straight-forward nomograph format was designed. The new format can be used to estimate effective midflame wind speed when wind direction is not upslope and to estimate fire behavior in non-heading directions. Nomographs for the original 13 fuel models have been created in the new format.

USDA Forest Service Gen. Tech. Rep. RMRS-GTR-192. 2007

9

References

Albini, F. A. 1976. Estimating wildfire behavior and effects. Gen. Tech. Rep. INT-30. Ogden, Utah: Department of Agriculture, Forest Service, Intermountain Forest and Range Experiment Station. 92 p.

Albini, F. A.; Baughman, R. G. 1979. Estimating windspeeds for predicting wildland fire behavior. Res. Pap. INT-221. Ogden, Utah: U.S. Department of Agriculture, Forest Service, Intermountain Forest and Range Experiment Station. 12 p.

Anderson, D. H.; Catchpole, E. A.; de Mestre, N. J.; Parkes, T. 1982. Modelling the spread of grass fires. J. Aust. Math. Soc. (Ser. B) 23: 451-466.

Anderson, H. E. 1982. Aids to determining fuel models for estimating fire behavior. Gen. Tech. Rep. INT-122. Ogden, UT: U.S. Department of Agriculture, Forest Service, Intermountain Forest and Range Experiment Station. 22 p.

Andrews, P. L. 1986. BEHAVE: Fire behavior prediction and fuel modeling system — BURN Subsystem, Part 1. Gen. Tech. Rep. INT-194. Ogden, UT: U.S. Department of Agriculture, Forest Service, Intermountain Forest and Range Experiment Station. 130 p.

Burgan, R. E. 1979. Estimating live fuel moisture for the 1978 national fire danger rating system. GTR-INT-226, USDA Forest Service, Ogden, UT. 17 p.

Byram, G. M. 1959. Combustion of forest fuels. In: Forest fire: Control and use, 2nd edition. New York, NY: McGraw-Hill: chapter 1, 61-89.

Catchpole, E. A.; Alexander, M. E.; Gill, A. M. 1992. Elliptical-fire perimeter- and area-intensity distributions. Can. J. For. Res. 22: 968-972.

Catchpole, E. A.; de Mestre, N. J.; Gill, A. M. 1982. Intensity of fire at its perimeter. Aust. For. Res. 12: 47-54.

Jolly, W. M. 2005. Sensitivity of a fire behavior model to changes in live fuel moisture. In: Proceedings of the Sixth Symposium on Fire and Forest Meteorology, Canmore, AB, Canada.

Rothermel, R. C. 1972. A mathematical model for predicting fire spread in wildland fuels. Res. Pap. INT-115. Ogden, UT: U.S. Department of Agriculture, Forest Service, Intermountain Forest and Range Experiment Station. 40 p.

Scott, J. H.; R. E. Burgan. 2005. Standard fire behavior fuel models: a comprehensive set for use with Rothermel's surface fire spread model. Gen. Tech. Rep. RMRS-GTR-153. Ft. Collins, CO: U.S. Department of Agriculture, Forest Service, Rocky Mountain Research Station. 72 p.

10

USDA Forest Service Gen. Tech. Rep. RMRS-GTR-192. 2007

Appendix A—Fire Behavior in Non-heading Spread Directions

Assuming fire spreads as a simple ellipse (Anderson and others 1982), the fraction of headfire rate of spread (R_ψ/R_{head}) expected for a flame front oriented any direction with respect to the direction of maximum spread (fig. A1) can be estimated following Catchpole and others (1982) as:

$$R_\psi \Big/ R_{head} = c * COS(\psi) + \sqrt{a^2 * COS^2(\psi) + b^2 * SIN^2(\psi)} \qquad [1]$$

where ψ is the normal angle (fig. A1), and following Catchpole and others (1992)

$$a = \frac{1}{1 + \sqrt{1 - L_B^{-2}}} \qquad [2]$$

$$b = \frac{a}{L_B} \qquad [3]$$

$$c = a\sqrt{1 - L_B^{-2}} \qquad [4]$$

where L_B is the length-to-breadth ratio of the ellipse, which can be estimated as a simple function of effective midflame wind speed (Andrews 1986)

$$L_B = 1 + 0.25U_m \qquad [5]$$

where U_m is the effective midflame wind speed. Rate of spread for flame front oriented in any direction relative to the direction of maximum spread (R_ψ) is therefore

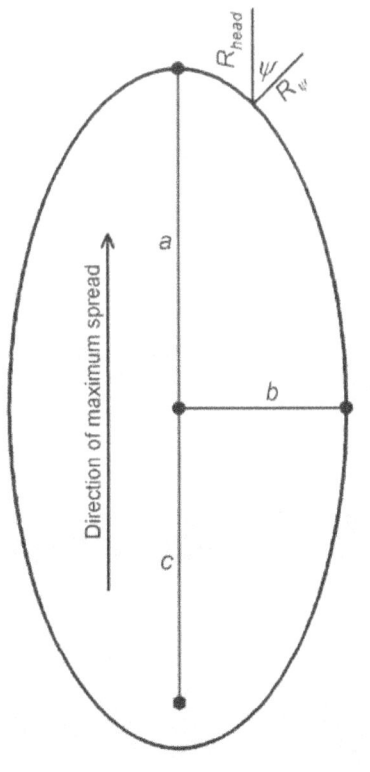

Figure A1—Elliptical dimensions *a*, *b*, and *c*, and graphical illustration of calculations for non-heading fire behavior. Length-to-breadth ratio (L_B) = 2 for the ellipse shown. The point shown on the ellipse is oriented 45 degrees from the heading direction. At that point, *a* = 0.536, *b* = 0.268, *c* = 0.464, $R_{fraction}$ = 0.752, and $FL_{fraction}$ = 0.877.

$$R_\psi = R_{head} * \left(\frac{R_\psi}{R_{head}} \right)$$

[6]

where R_{head} is the spread rate in the direction of maximum spread.

Using Byram's (1959) relationship between flame length and fireline intensity, the fraction of head fire flame length that would occur at the same flame front orientation, FL_ψ / FL_{head}, is

$$\left(\frac{FL_\psi}{FL_{head}} \right) = \frac{0.45 \left(I_{head} * \left(\frac{R_\psi}{R_{head}} \right) \right)^{0.46}}{0.45 \left(I_{head} \right)^{0.46}}$$

[7]

which reduces to

$$FL_\psi = FL_{head} \left(\frac{R_\psi}{R_{head}} \right)^{0.46}$$

[8]

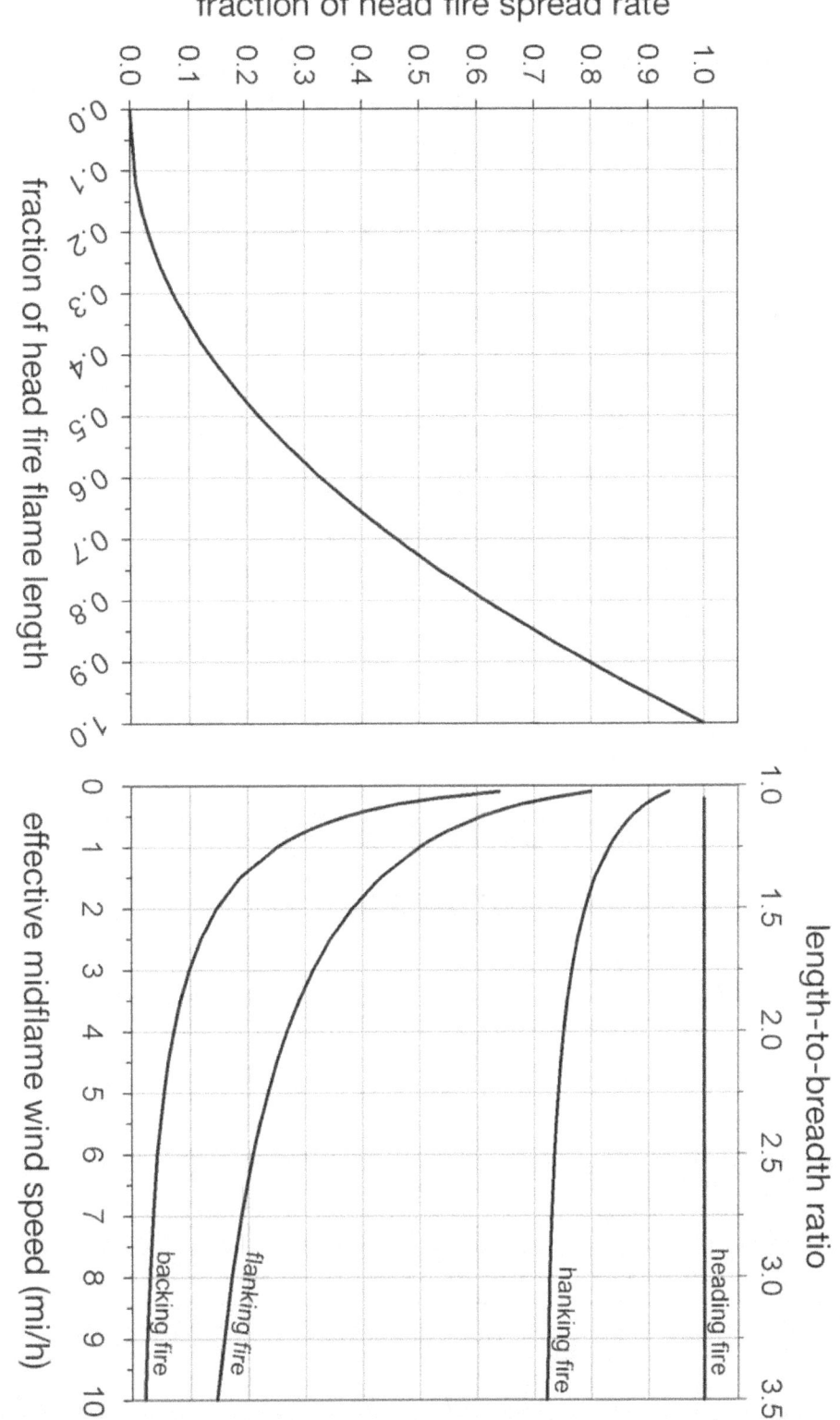

USDA Forest Service Gen. Tech. Rep. RMRS-GTR-192. 2007

13

Appendix B—Nomographs

Fire Behavior Nomograph Worksheet				
analyst name:				
project name:				
projection date and time:				
notes:	**Projection Point**			notes:
	A	**B**	**C**	
Fuel and Moisture				
(1) Fuel model				category
(2) dead woody fuel moisture				percent
(3) live herbaceous fuel moisture				percent
(4) live woody fuel moisture				percent
Wind and Slope				
(5) slope steepness				percent
(6) canopy cover				percent
(7) 20-ft wind speed				mi/h
(8) Wind Adjustment Factor				fraction (table 3 or 4)
(9) midflame wind speed				mi/h (direct entry or [7] x [8])
(10) wind direction				degrees clockwise from upslope
Spread Direction				
(11) spread direction				(heading, hanking, flanking, or backing)
Results				
(12) effective midflame wind speed				mi/h
(13) direction of maximum spread				degrees clockwise from upslope
(14) head fire rate of spread				ch/h
(15) head fire flame length				ft
(16) length-to-breadth ratio				ratio
(17) fraction of head fire rate of spread				fraction
(18) fraction of head fire flame length				fraction
(19) rate of spread in spread direction				ch/h ([14] x [17])
(20) flame length in spread direction				ft ([15] x [18])

USDA Forest Service Gen. Tech. Rep. RMRS-GTR-192. 2007

USDA Forest Service Gen. Tech. Rep. RMRS-GTR-192. 2007

15

FB1 (1)

low wind speeds

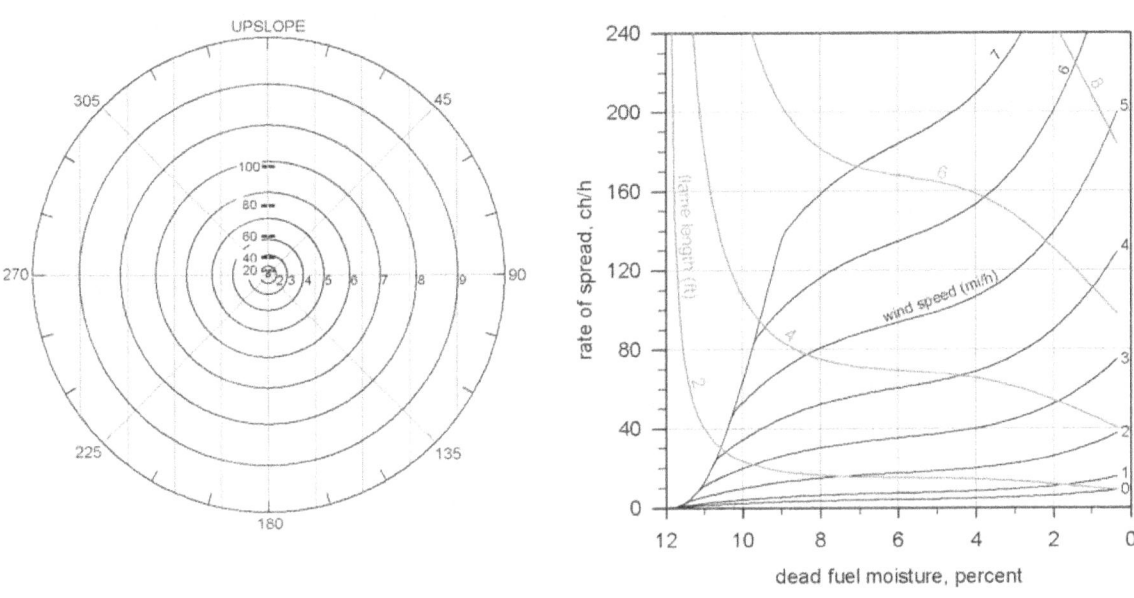

high wind speeds

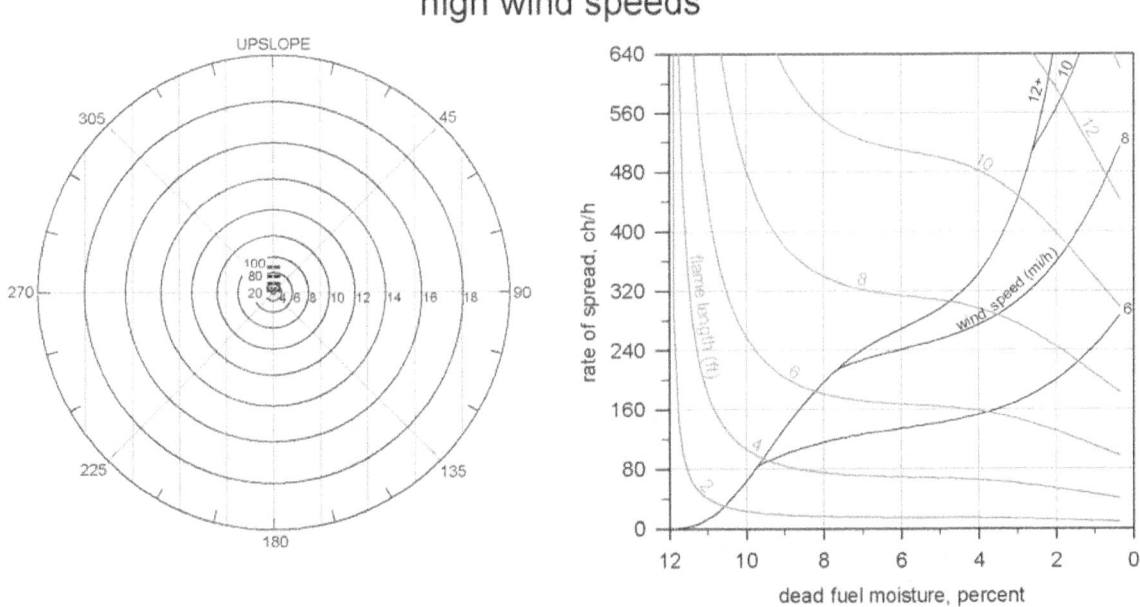

USDA Forest Service Gen. Tech. Rep. RMRS-GTR-192. 2007

17

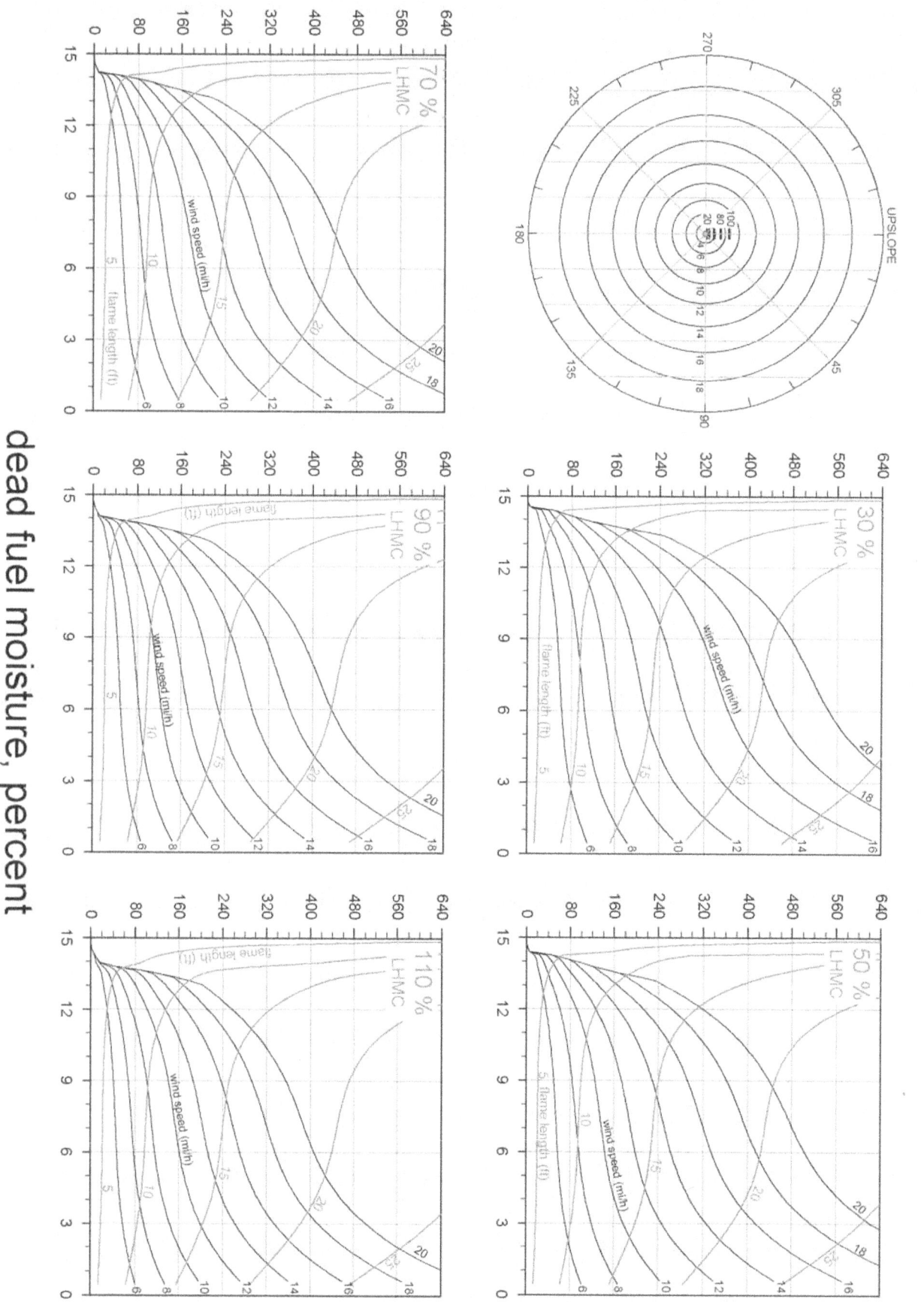

rate of spread, ch/h

dead fuel moisture, percent

FB2 (2) - high wind speeds

USDA Forest Service Gen. Tech. Rep. RMRS-GTR-192. 2007

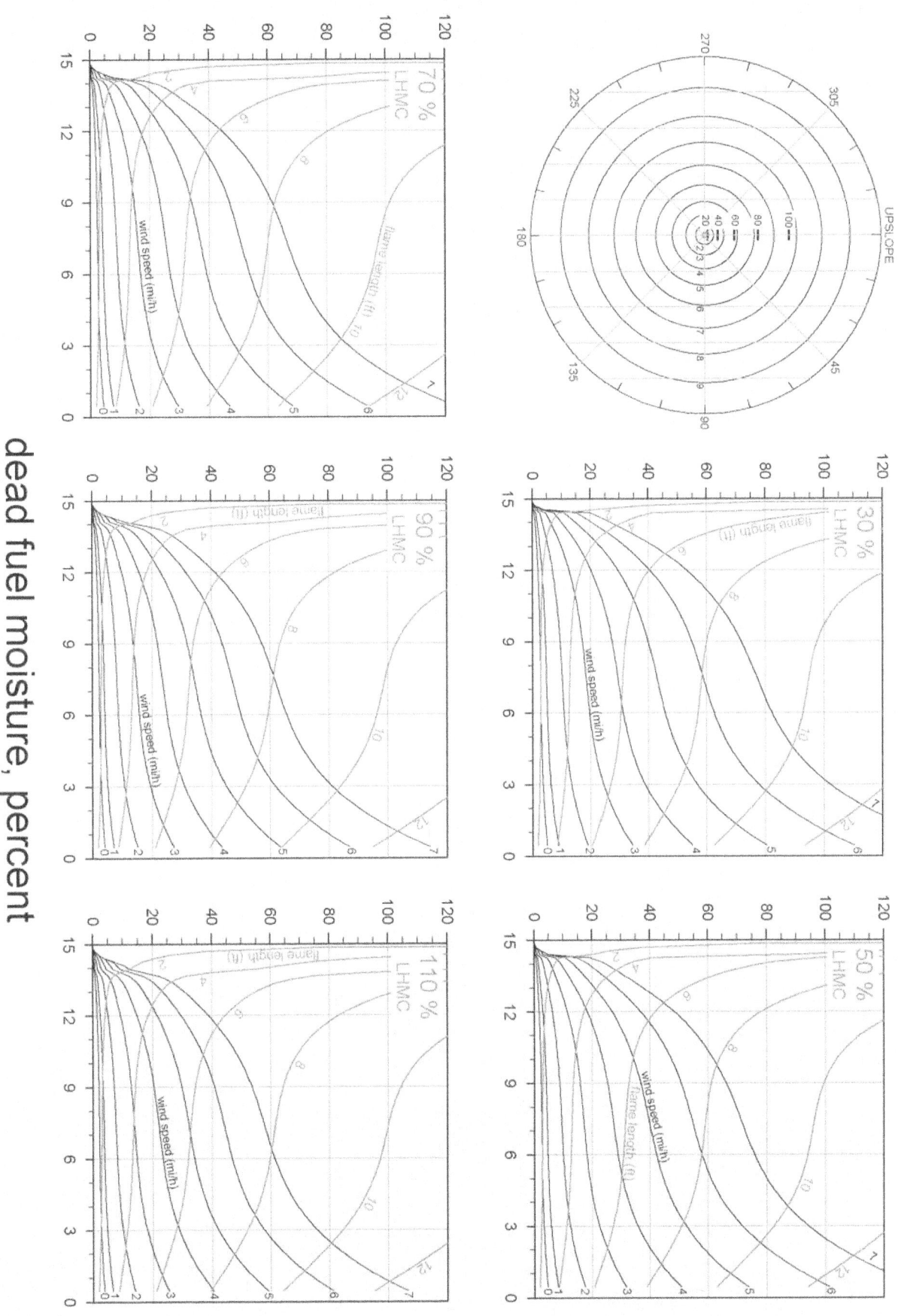

rate of spread, ch/h

dead fuel moisture, percent

FB2 (2) - low wind speeds

USDA Forest Service Gen. Tech. Rep. RMRS-GTR-192. 2007

19

FB3 (3)

low wind speeds

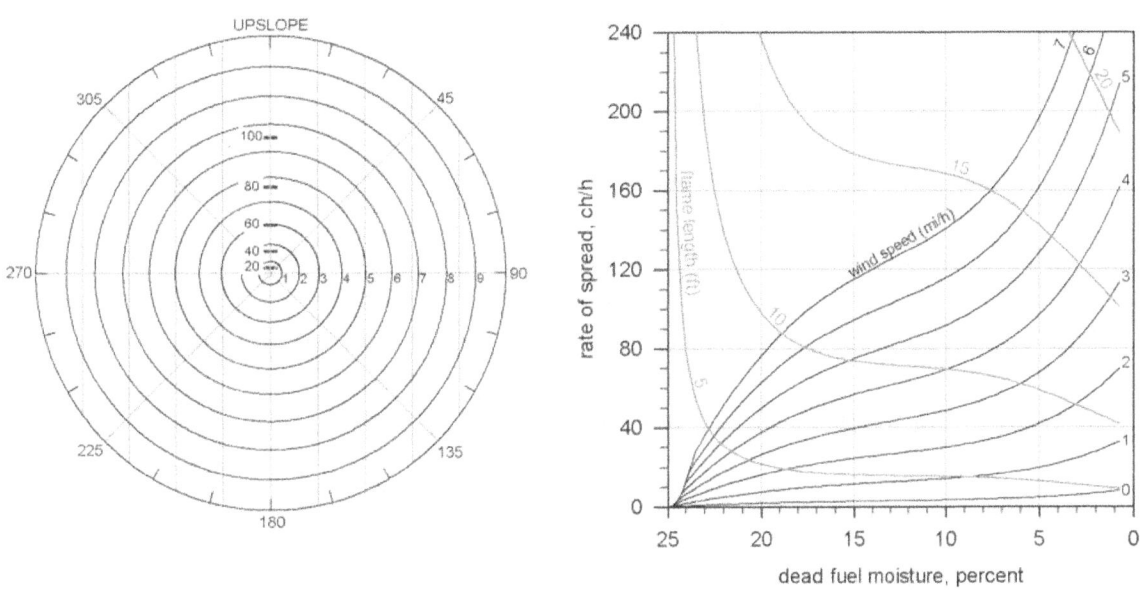

high wind speeds

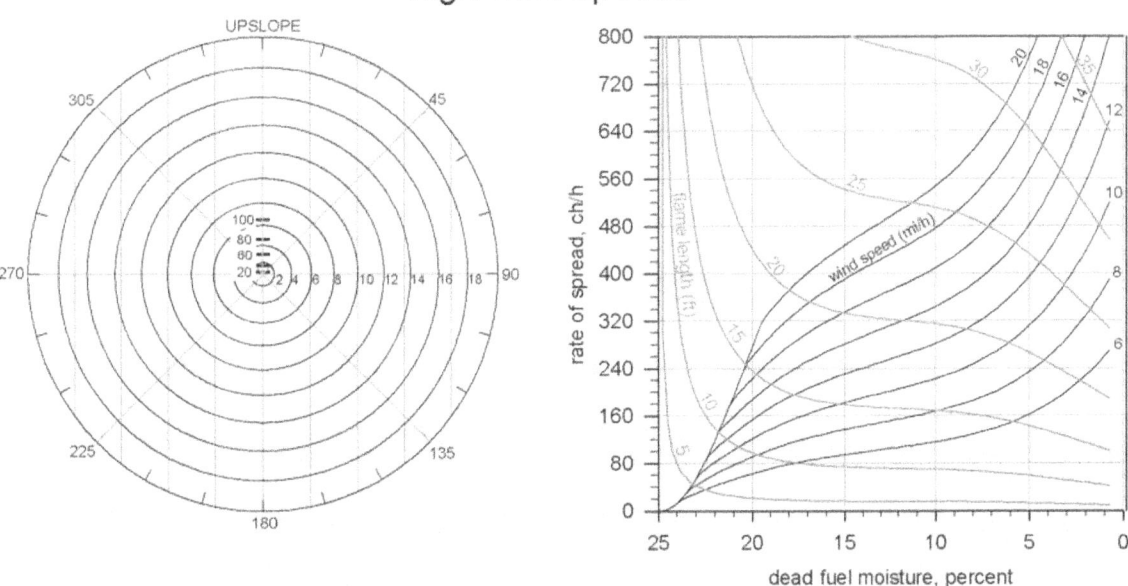

USDA Forest Service Gen. Tech. Rep. RMRS-GTR-192. 2007

21

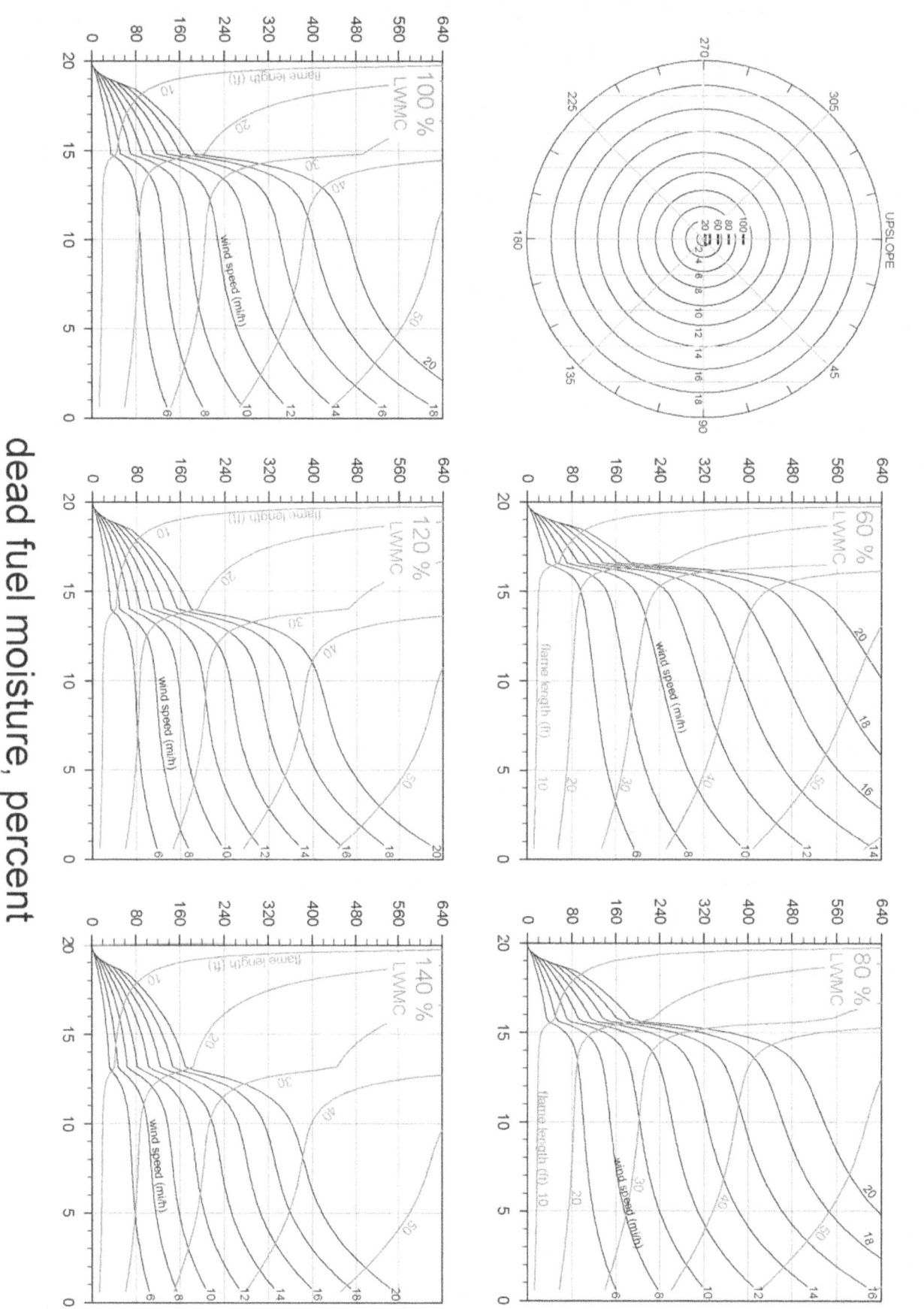

rate of spread, ch/h

dead fuel moisture, percent

FB4 (4)- high wind speeds

USDA Forest Service Gen. Tech. Rep. RMRS-GTR-192. 2007

rate of spread, ch/h

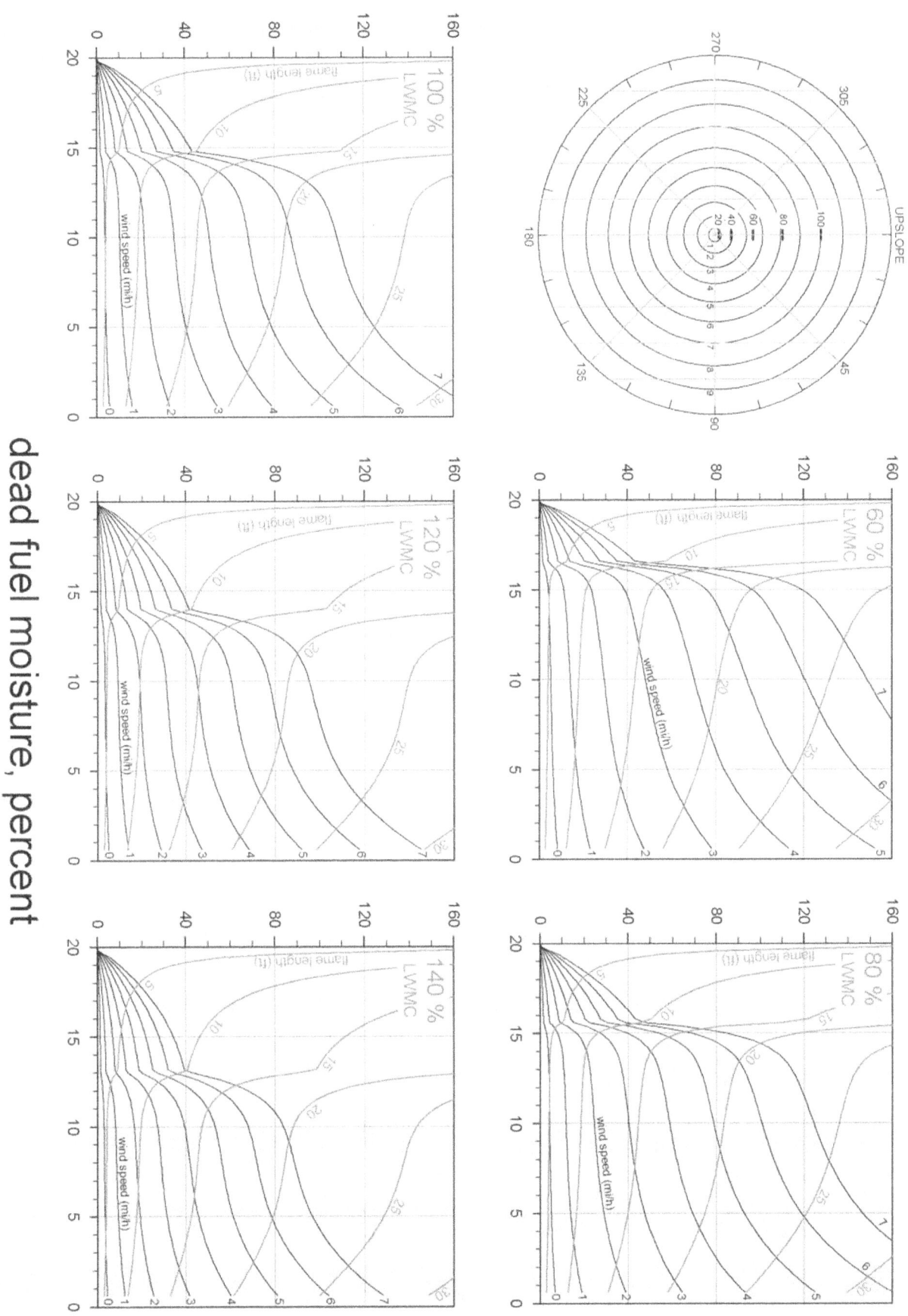

FB4 (4)- low wind speeds

dead fuel moisture, percent

USDA Forest Service Gen. Tech. Rep. RMRS-GTR-192. 2007

23

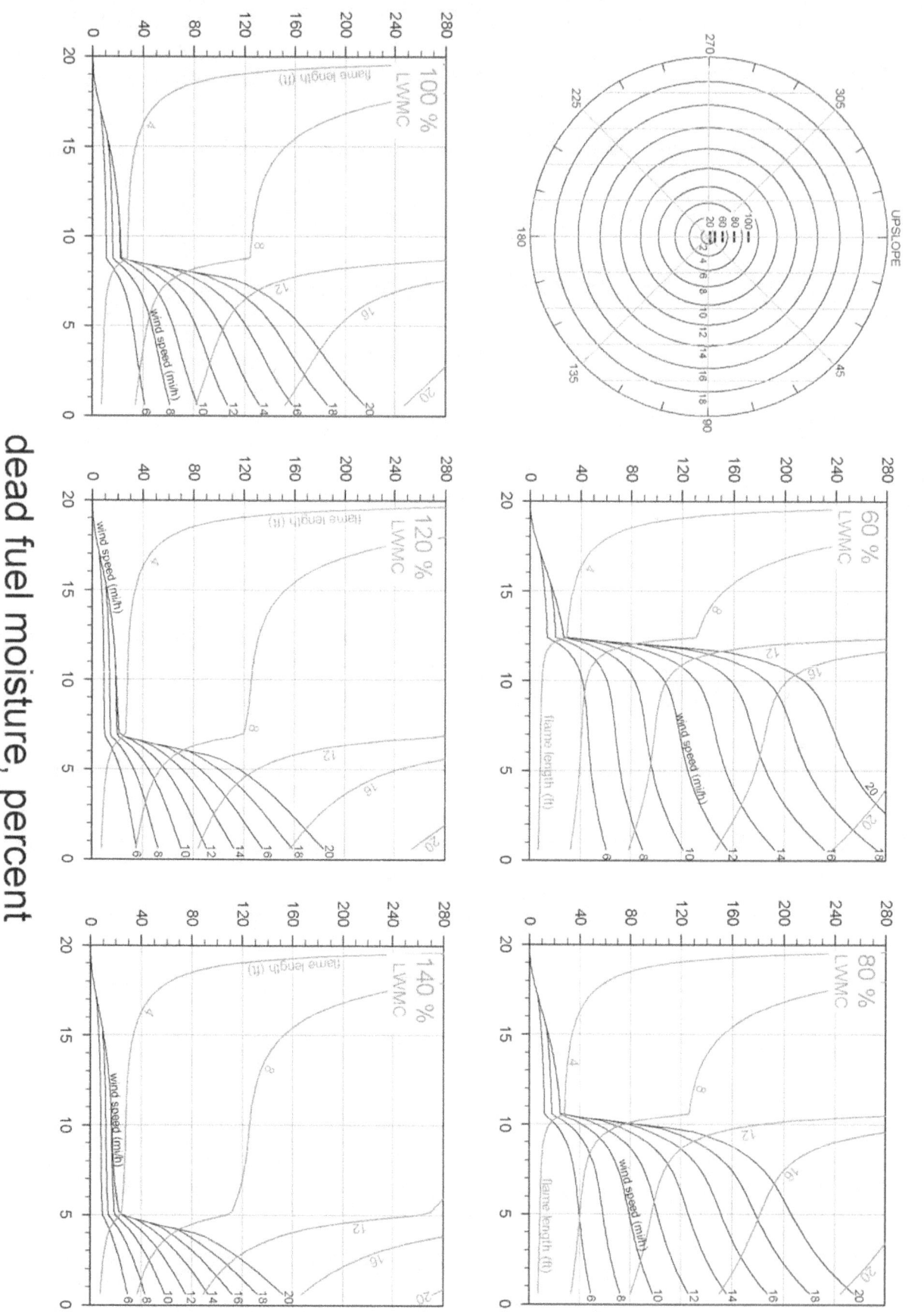

rate of spread, ch/h

dead fuel moisture, percent

FB5 (5)- high wind speeds

USDA Forest Service Gen. Tech. Rep. RMRS-GTR-192. 2007

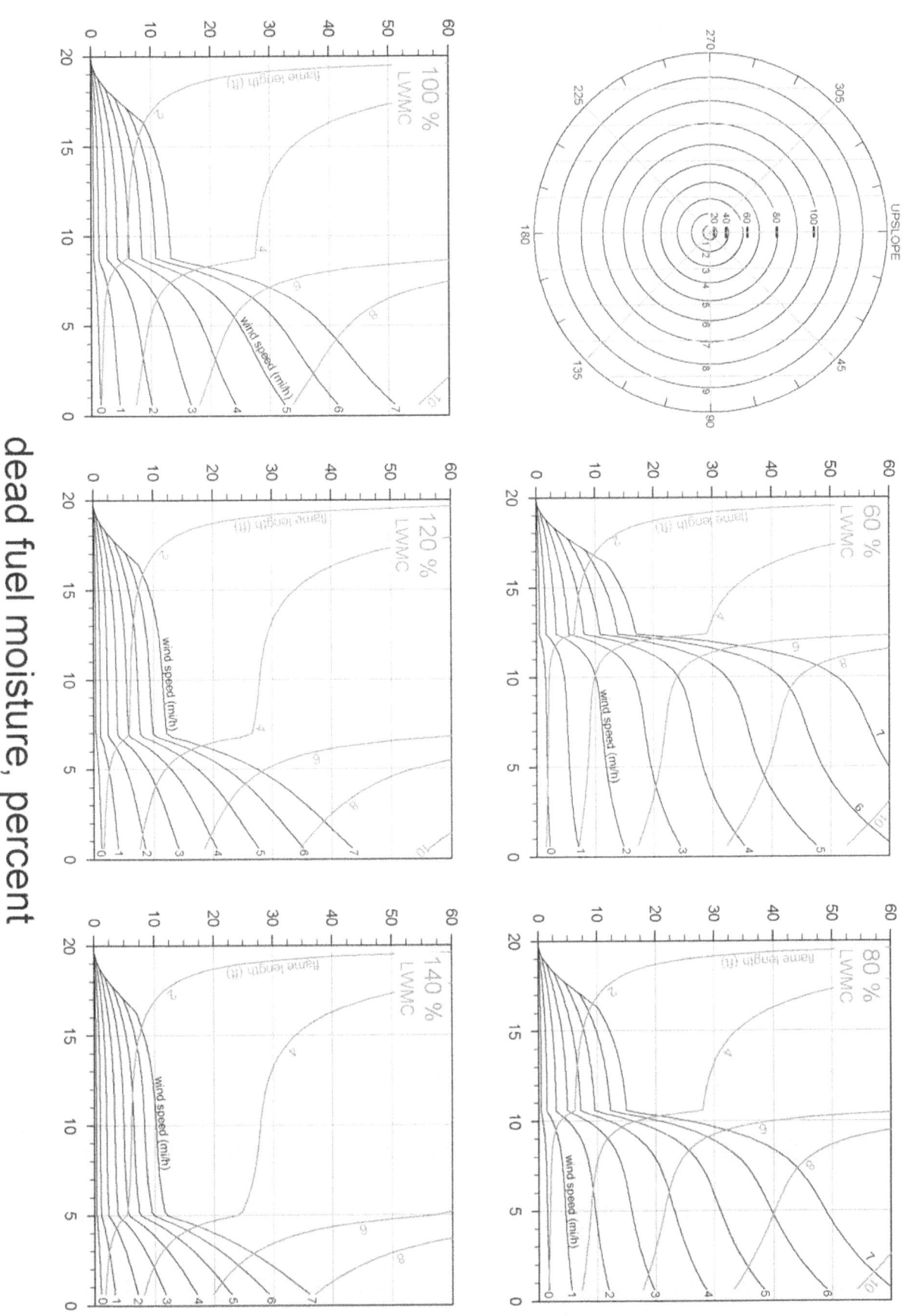

rate of spread, ch/h

dead fuel moisture, percent

FB5 (5)- low wind speeds

USDA Forest Service Gen. Tech. Rep. RMRS-GTR-192. 2007

25

FB6 (6)

low wind speeds

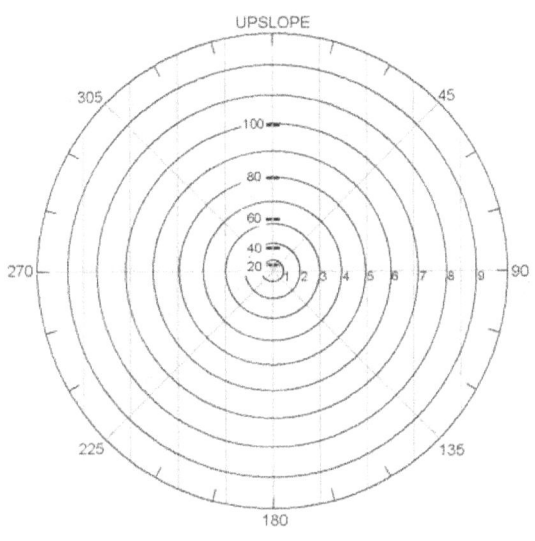

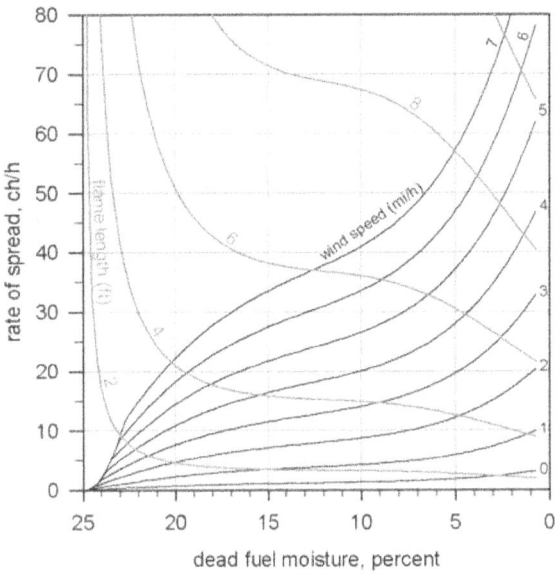

high wind speeds

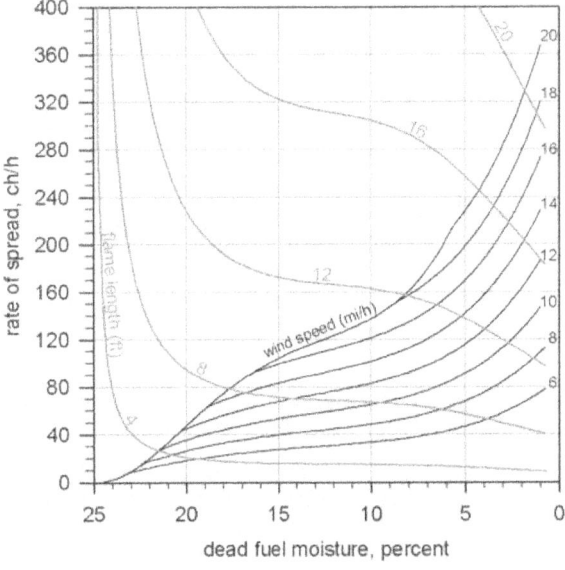

USDA Forest Service Gen. Tech. Rep. RMRS-GTR-192. 2007

27

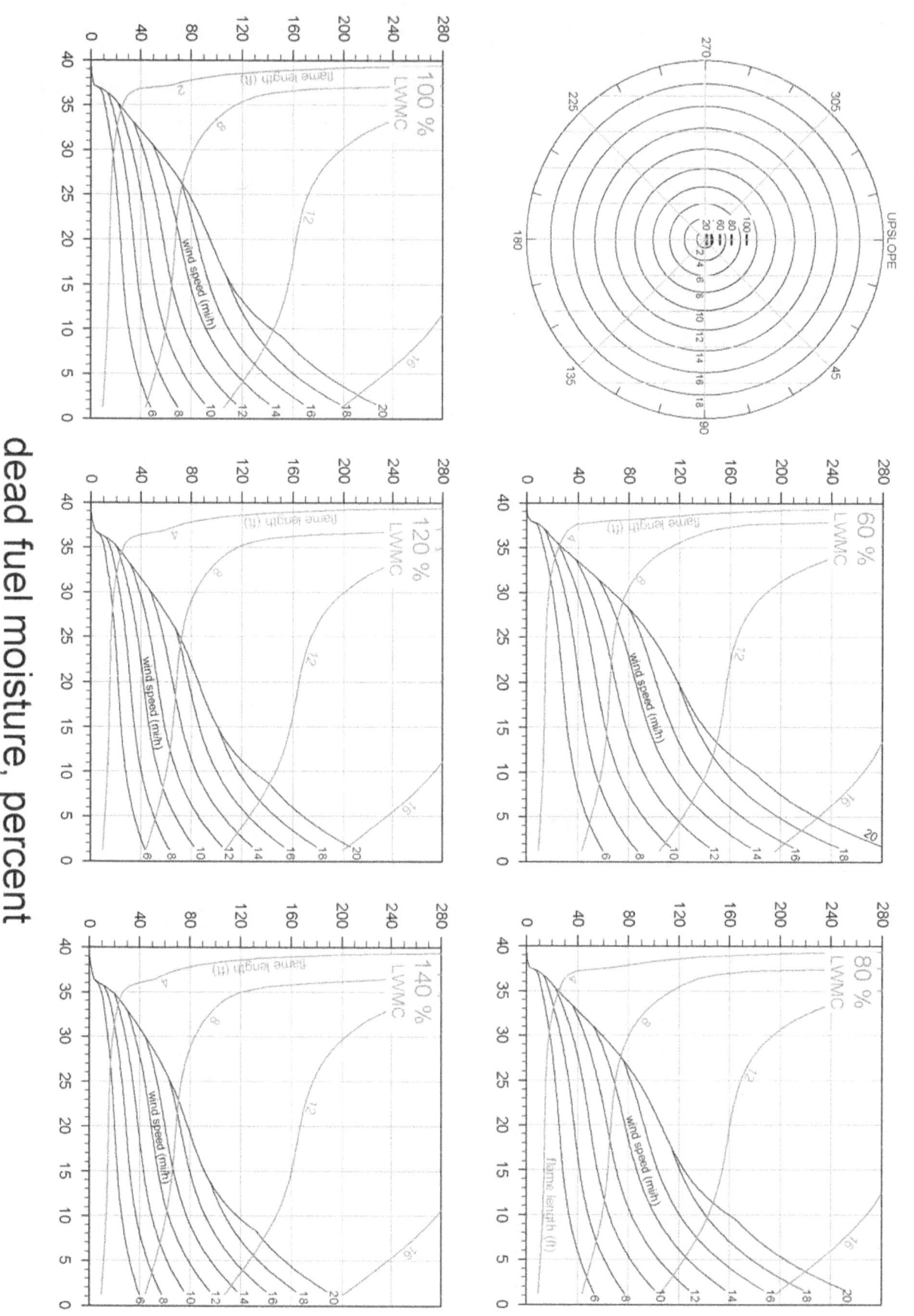

rate of spread, ch/h

dead fuel moisture, percent

FB7 (7)- high wind speeds

USDA Forest Service Gen. Tech. Rep. RMRS-GTR-192. 2007

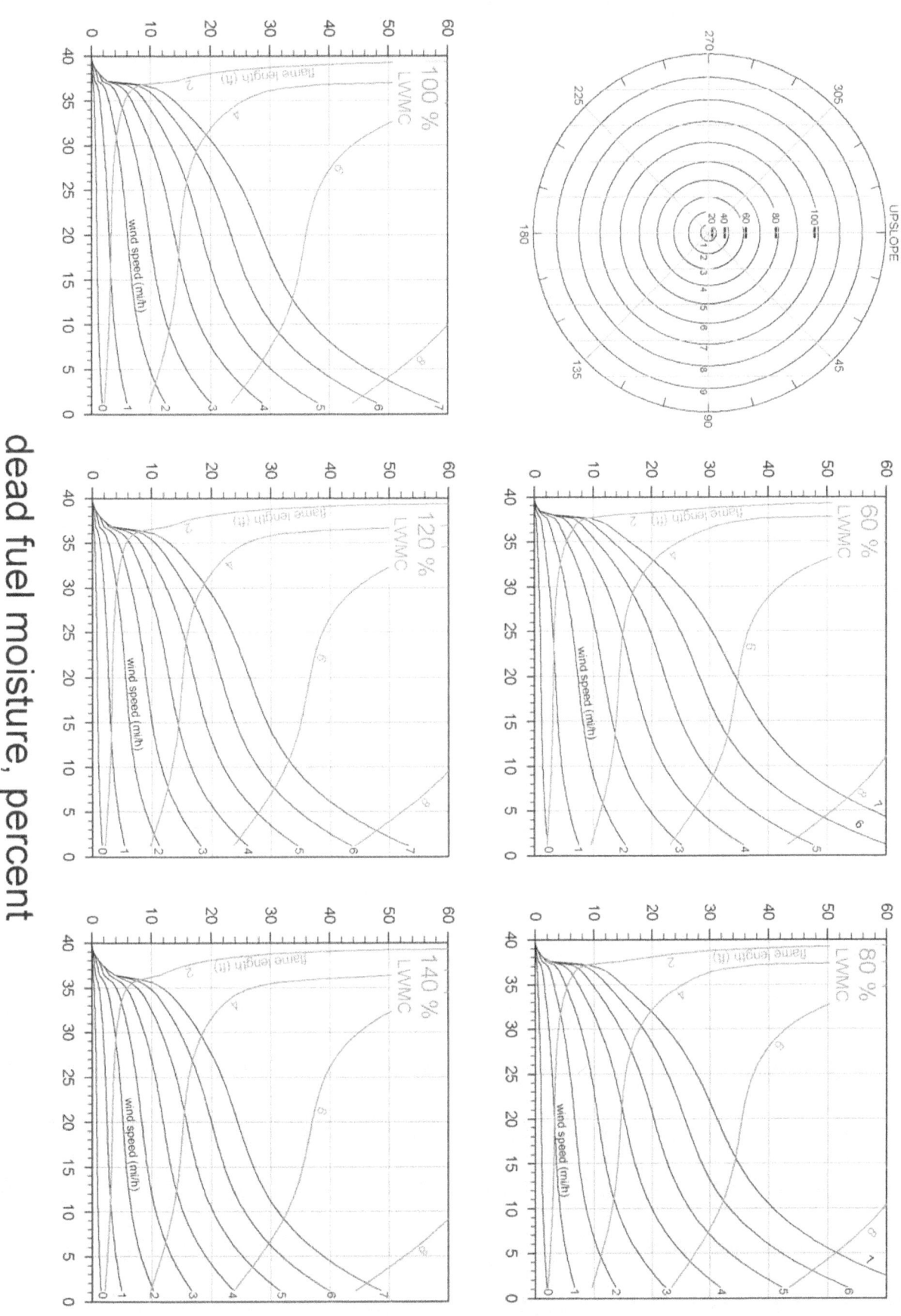

FB7 (7)- low wind speeds

rate of spread, ch/h

dead fuel moisture, percent

USDA Forest Service Gen. Tech. Rep. RMRS-GTR-192. 2007

29

FB8 (8)

low wind speeds

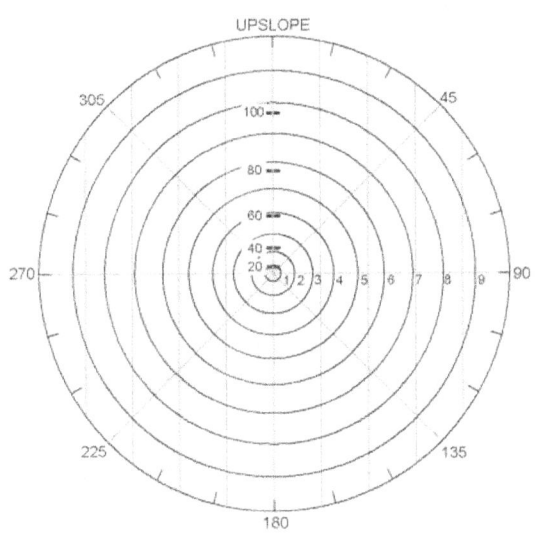

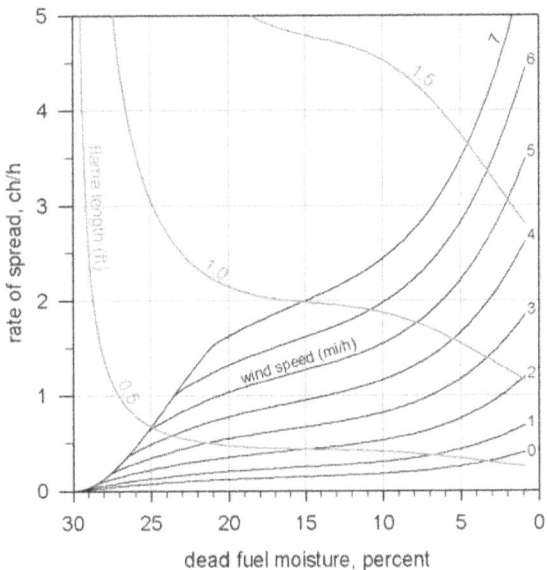

high wind speeds

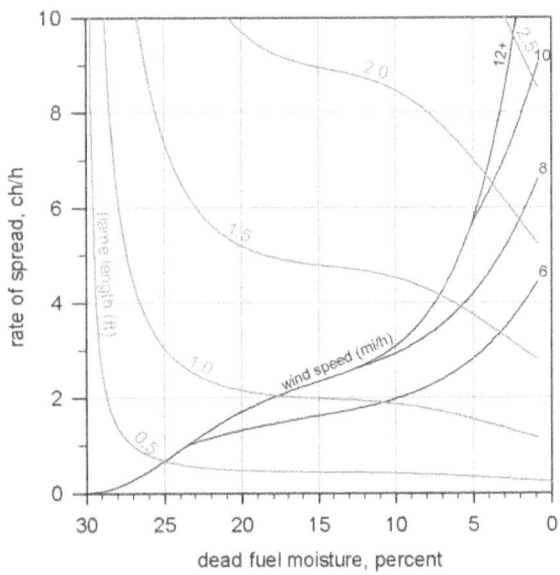

USDA Forest Service Gen. Tech. Rep. RMRS-GTR-192. 2007

31

FB9 (9)

low wind speeds

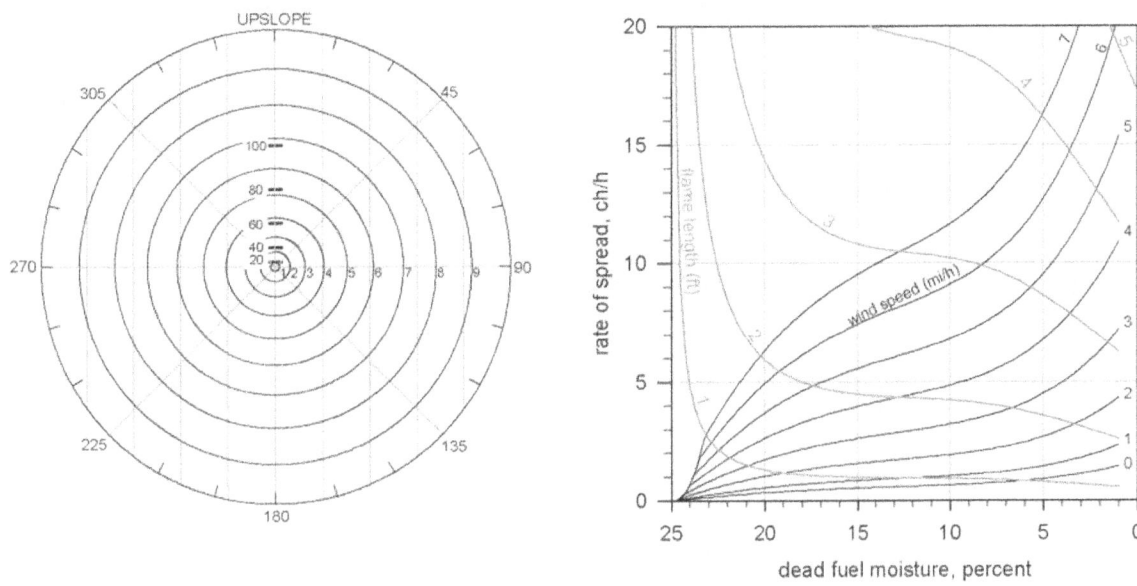

high wind speeds

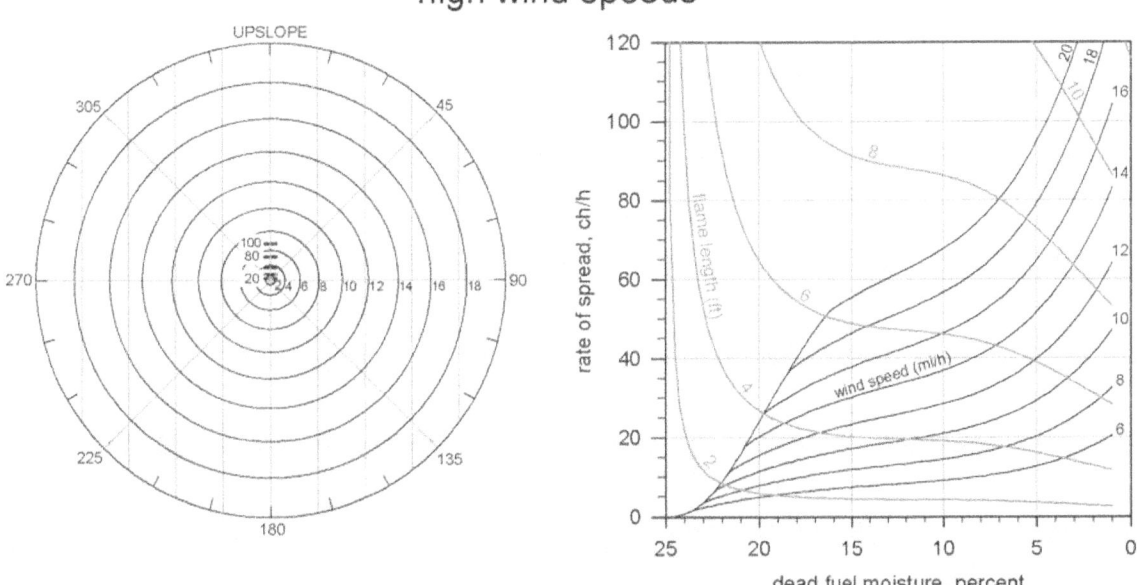

USDA Forest Service Gen. Tech. Rep. RMRS-GTR-192. 2007

33

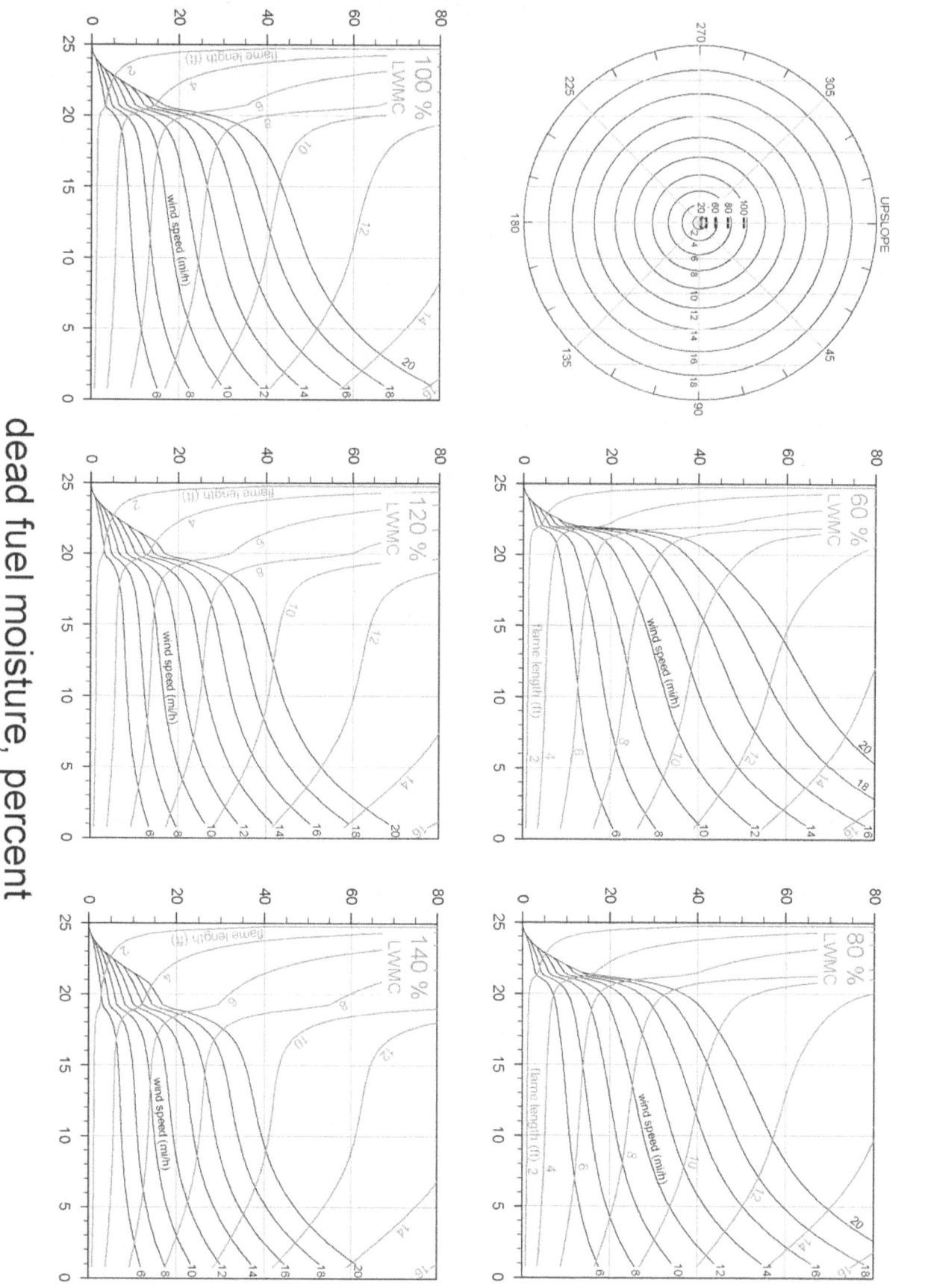

rate of spread, ch/h

dead fuel moisture, percent

FB10 (10)- high wind speeds

USDA Forest Service Gen. Tech. Rep. RMRS-GTR-192. 2007

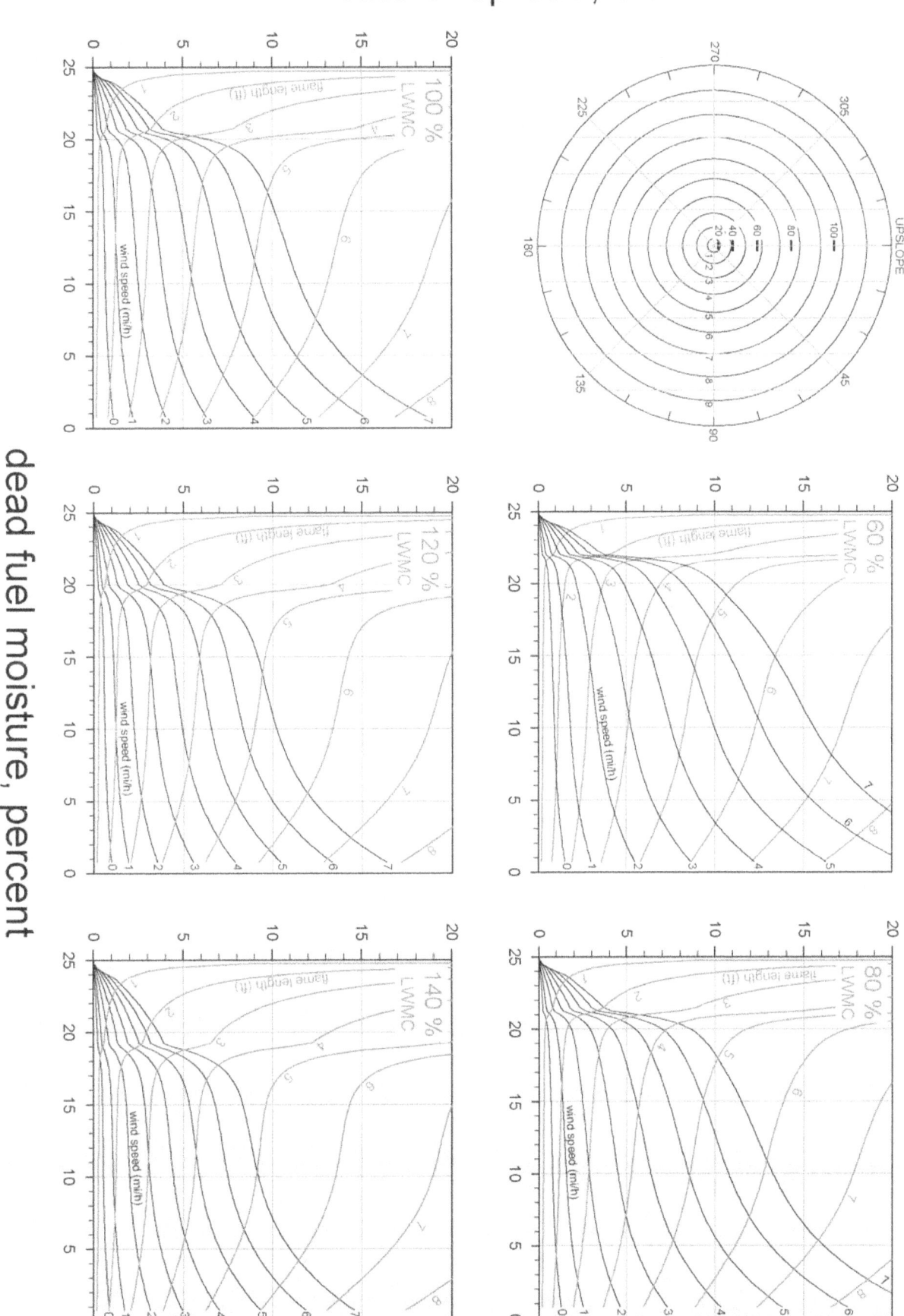

rate of spread, ch/h

dead fuel moisture, percent

FB10 (10)- low wind speeds

USDA Forest Service Gen. Tech. Rep. RMRS-GTR-192. 2007

35

FB11 (11)

low wind speeds

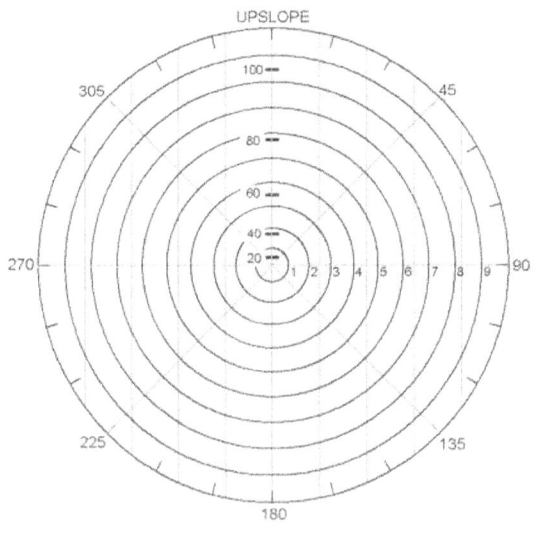

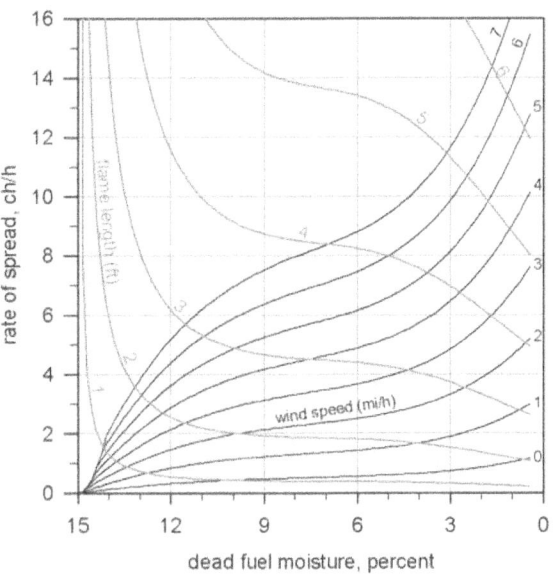

high wind speeds

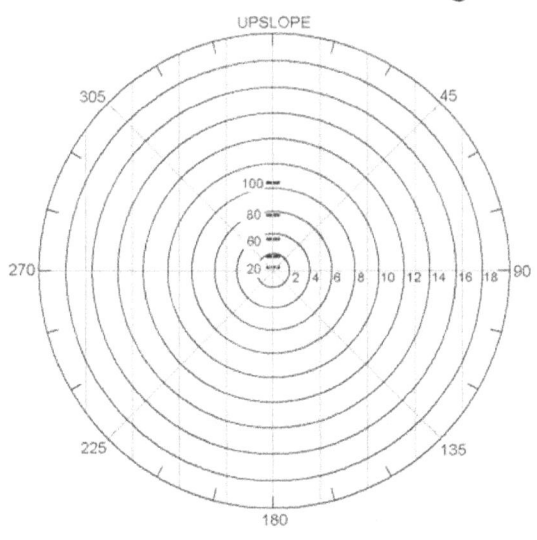

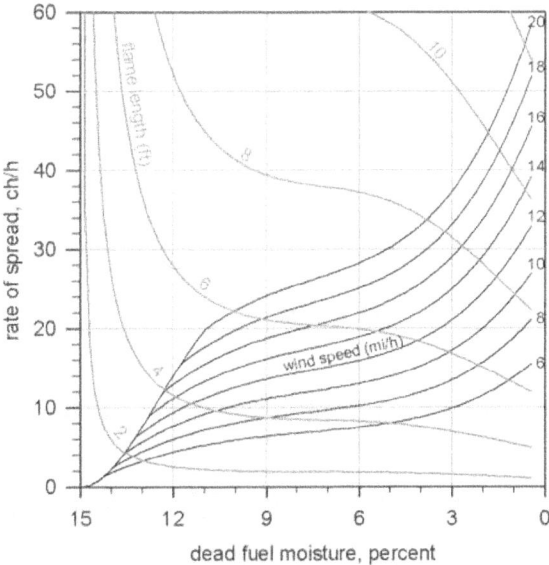

USDA Forest Service Gen. Tech. Rep. RMRS-GTR-192. 2007

37

38

USDA Forest Service Gen. Tech. Rep. RMRS-GTR-192. 2007

FB12 (12)

low wind speeds

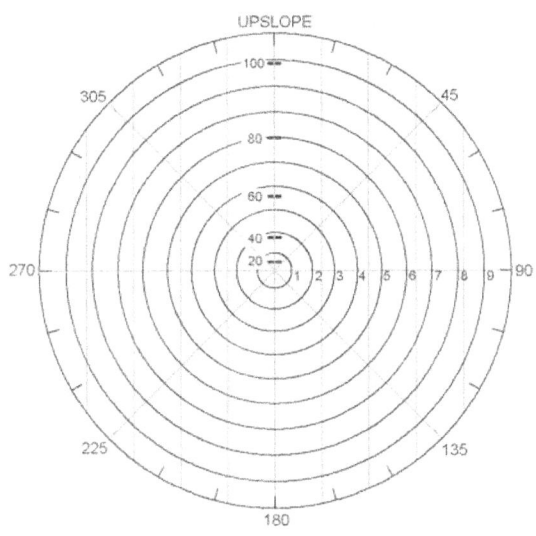

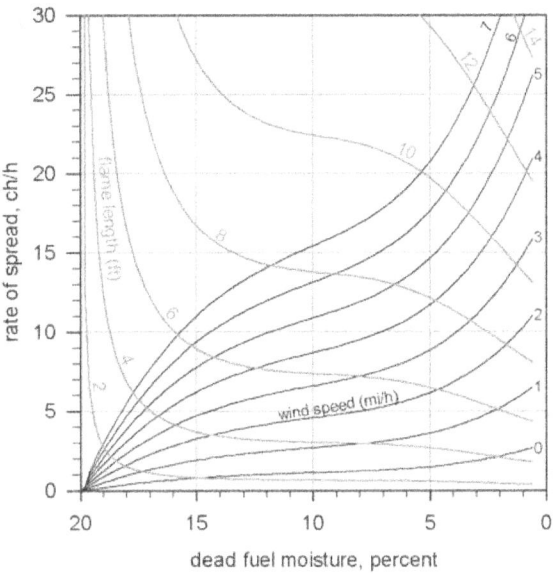

high wind speeds

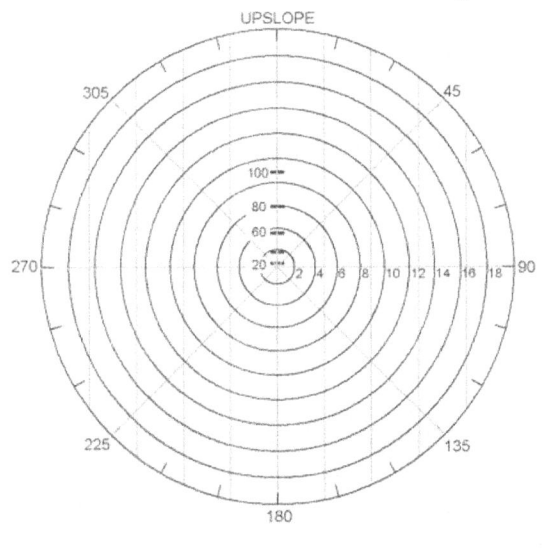

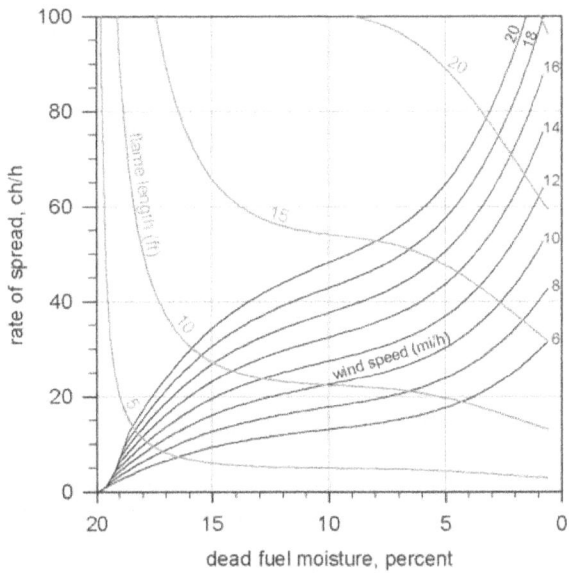

USDA Forest Service Gen. Tech. Rep. RMRS-GTR-192. 2007

39

40

USDA Forest Service Gen. Tech. Rep. RMRS-GTR-192. 2007

FB13 (13)

low wind speeds

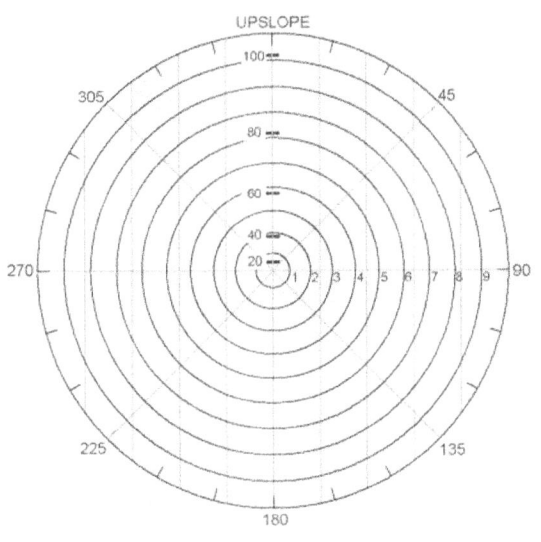

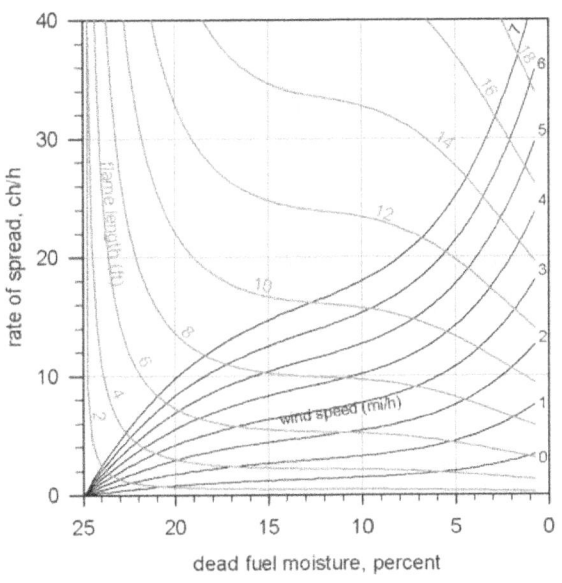

high wind speeds

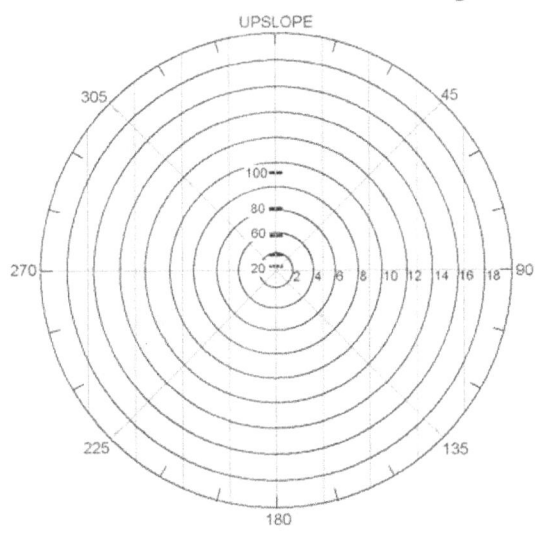

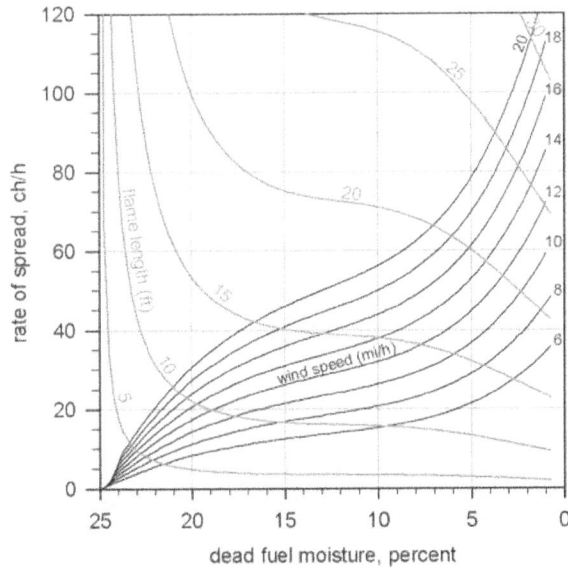

USDA Forest Service Gen. Tech. Rep. RMRS-GTR-192. 2007

41

Grass

USDA Forest Service Gen. Tech. Rep. RMRS-GTR-192. 2007

43

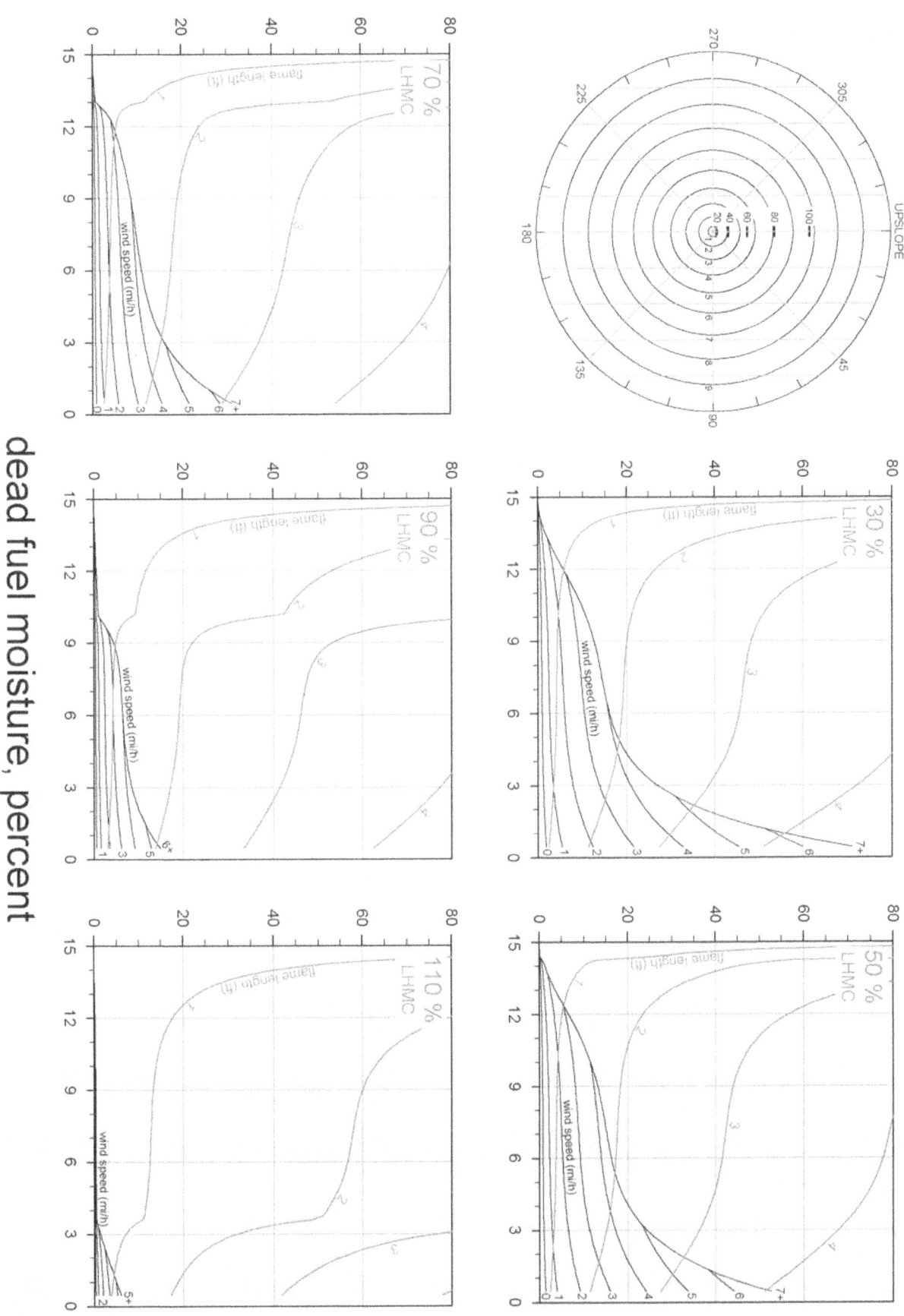

rate of spread, ch/h

GR1 (101) - all wind speeds

dead fuel moisture, percent

USDA Forest Service Gen. Tech. Rep. RMRS-GTR-192. 2007

45

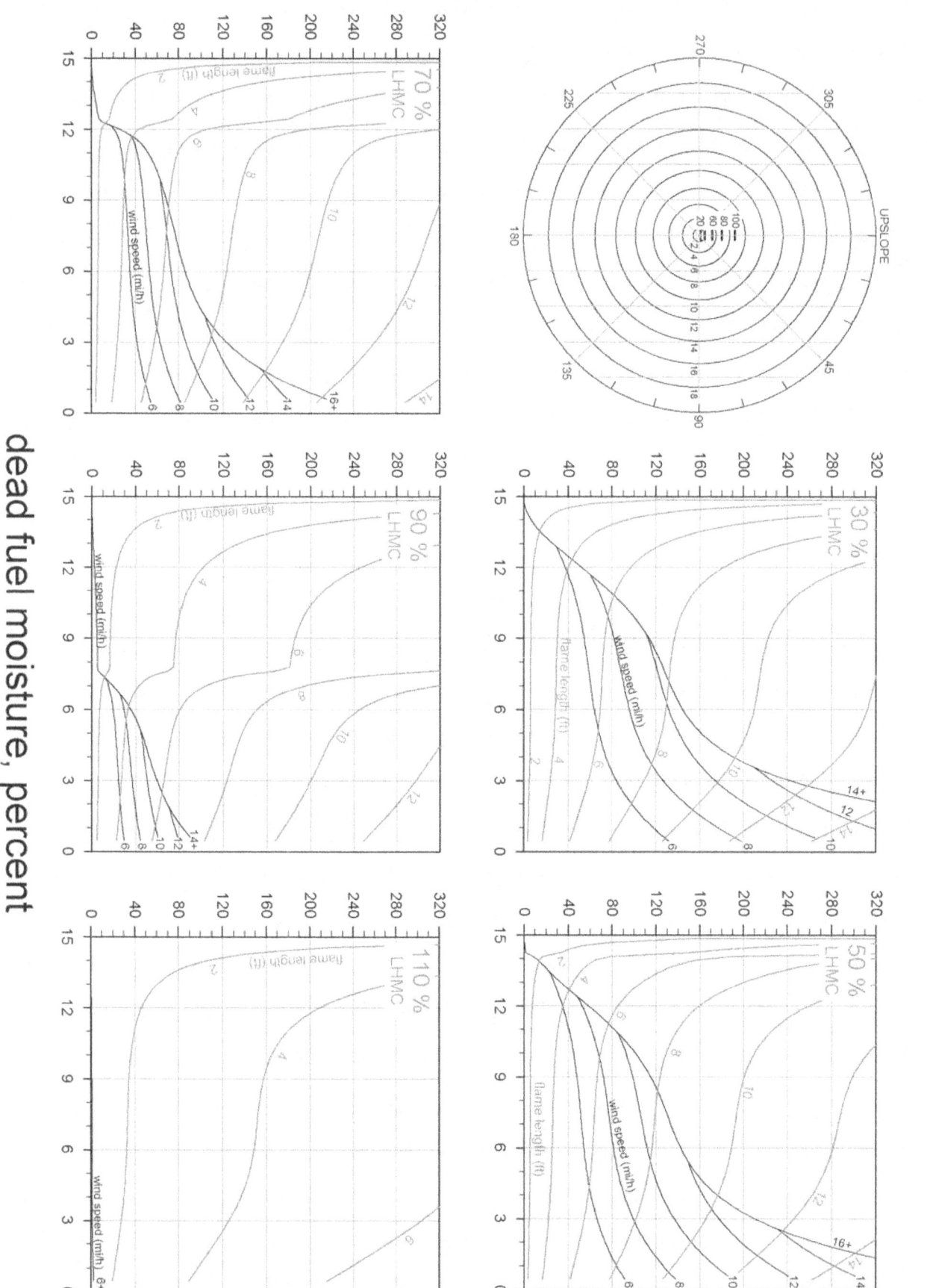

rate of spread, ch/h

dead fuel moisture, percent

GR2 (102)- high wind speeds

USDA Forest Service Gen. Tech. Rep. RMRS-GTR-192. 2007

rate of spread, ch/h

GR2 (102)- low wind speeds

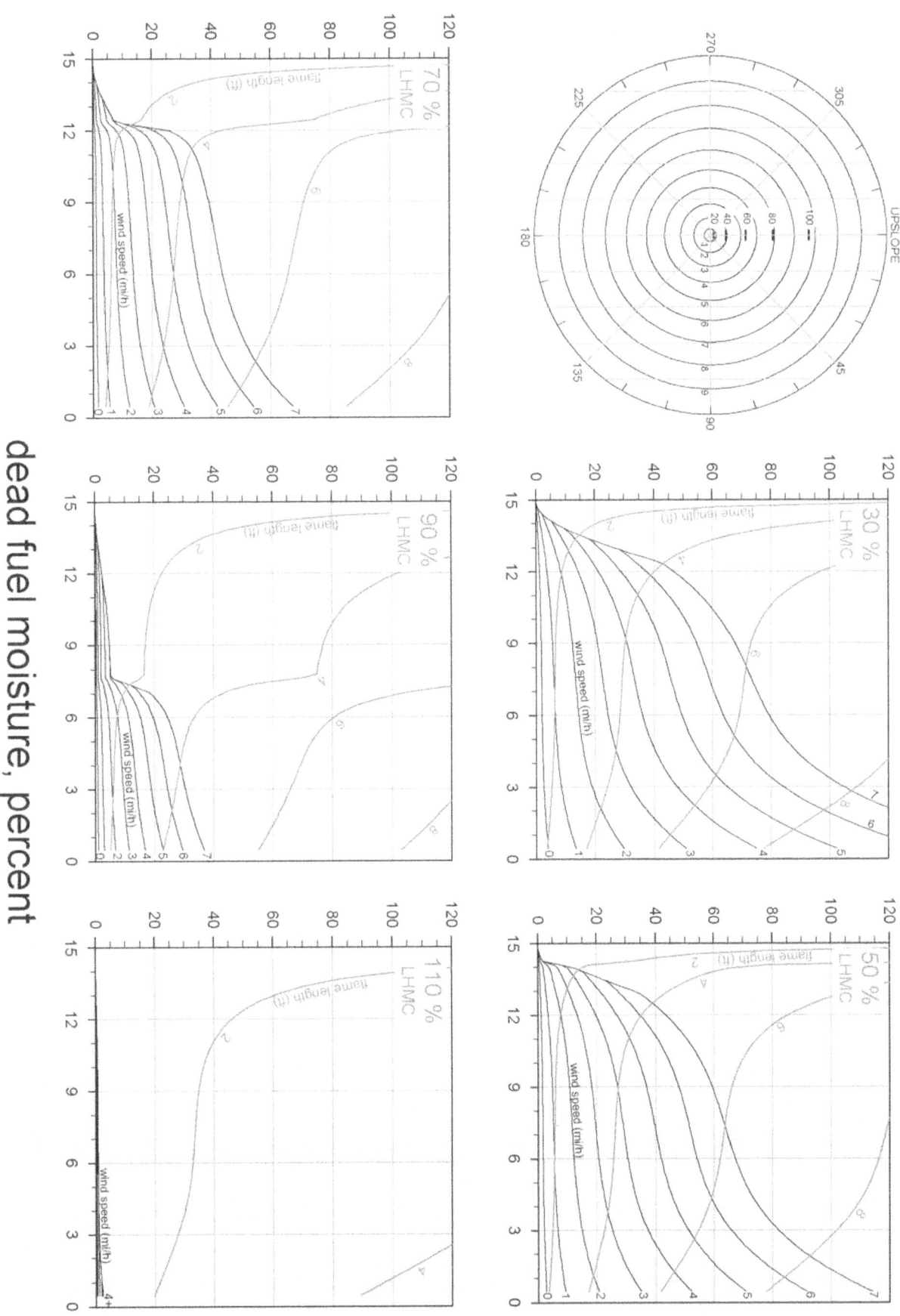

dead fuel moisture, percent

USDA Forest Service Gen. Tech. Rep. RMRS-GTR-192. 2007

47

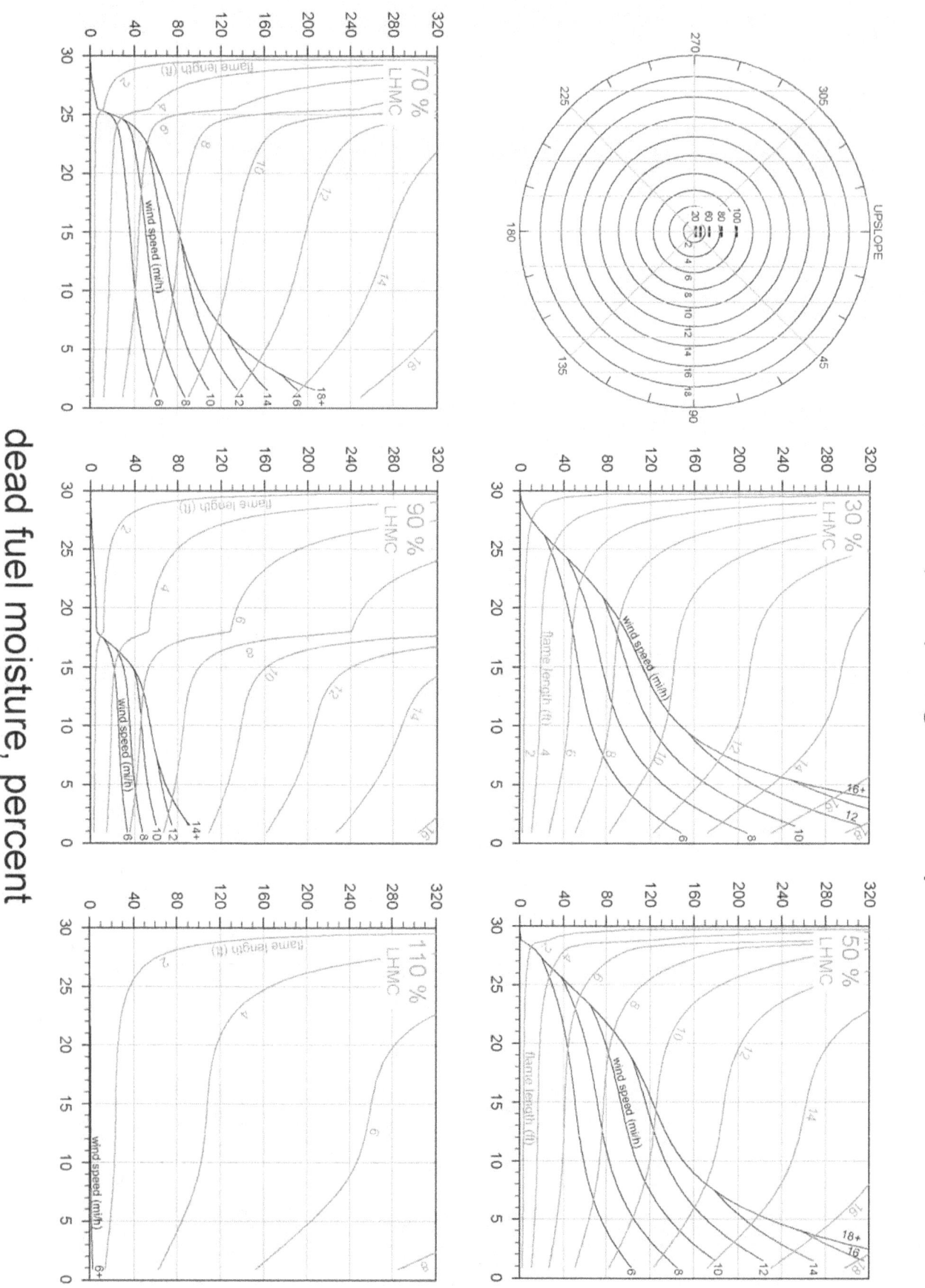

rate of spread, ch/h

dead fuel moisture, percent

GR3 (103)- high wind speeds

48

USDA Forest Service Gen. Tech. Rep. RMRS-GTR-192. 2007

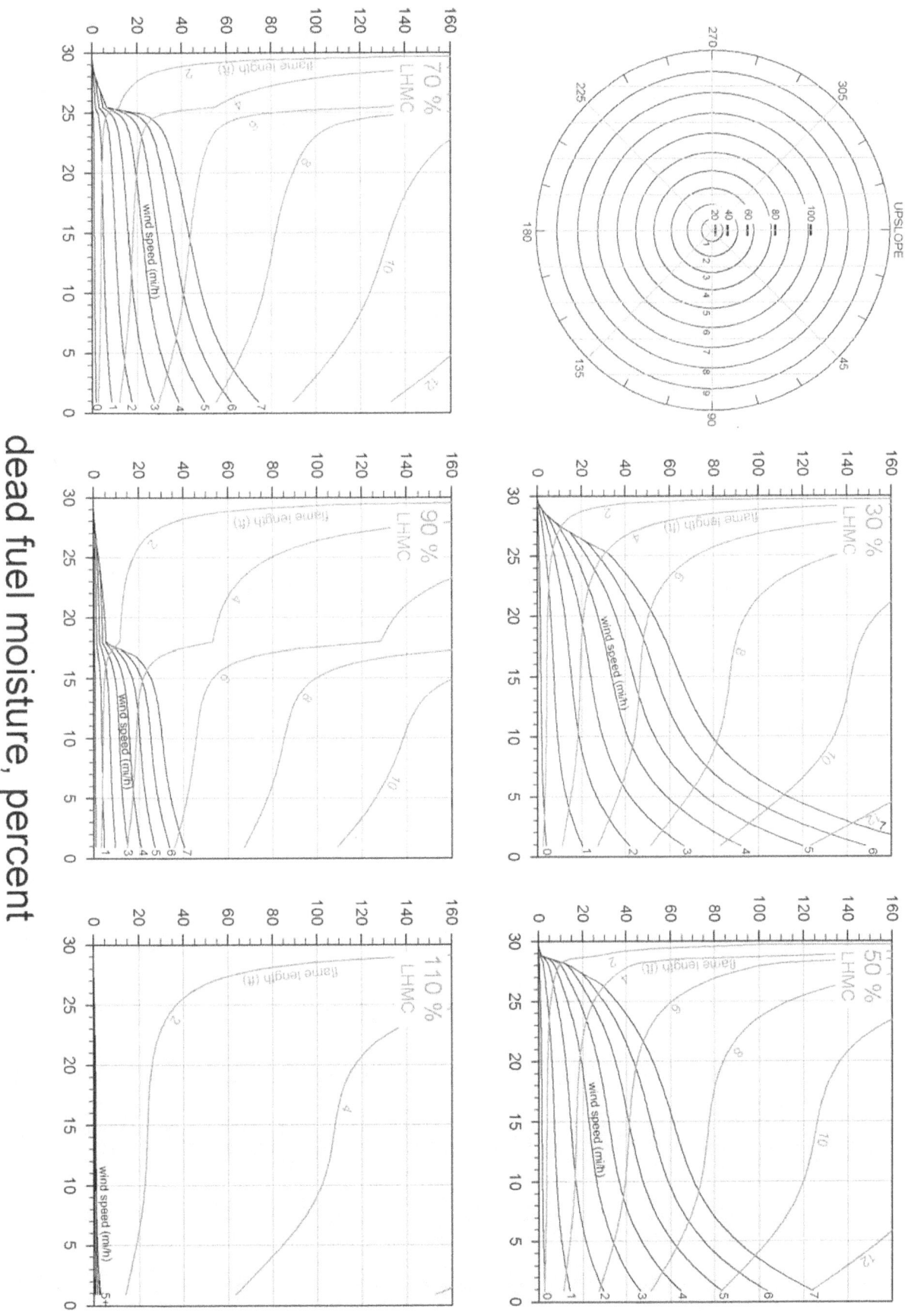

rate of spread, ch/h

dead fuel moisture, percent

GR3 (103) - low wind speeds

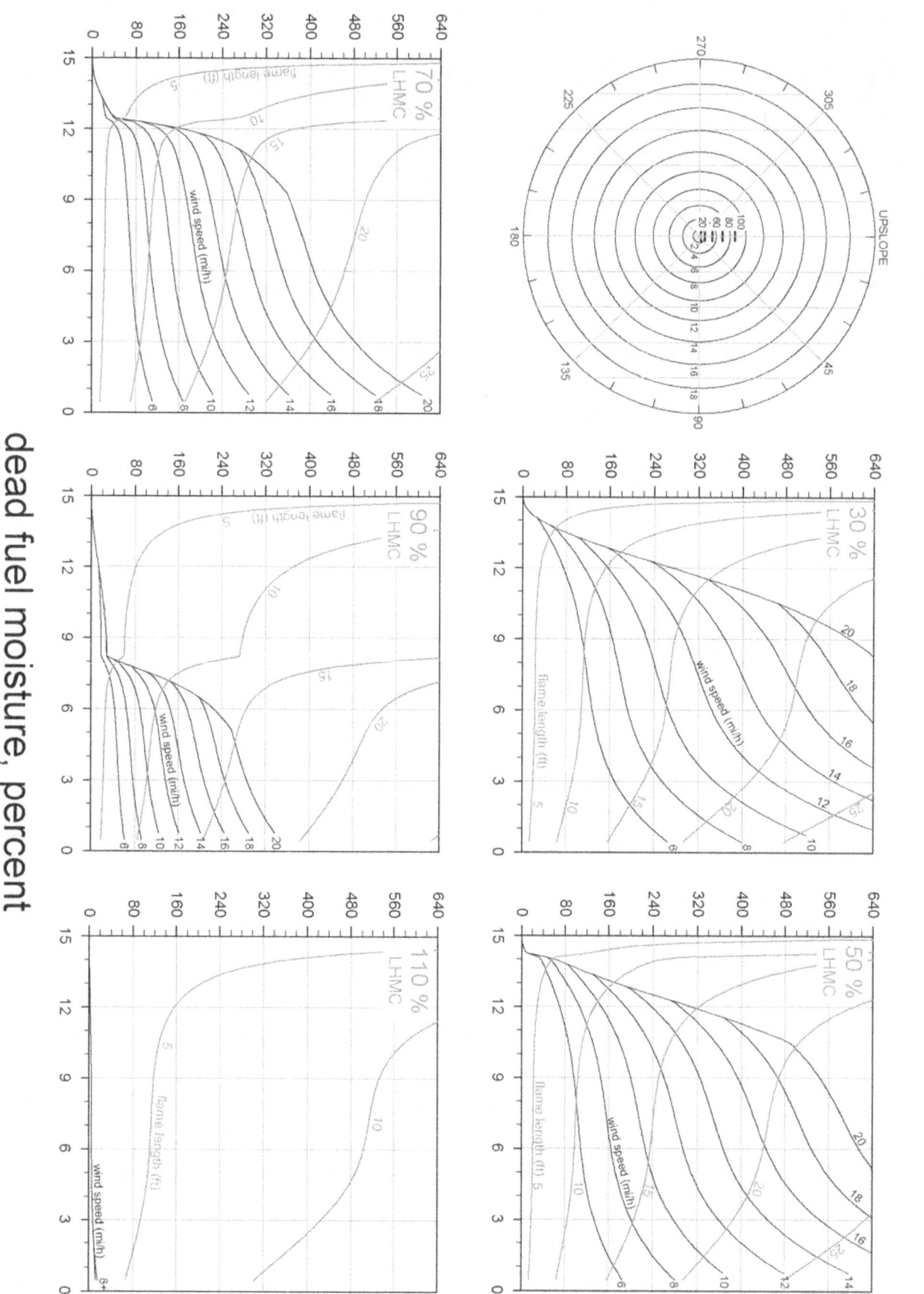

rate of spread, ch/h

dead fuel moisture, percent

GR4 (104)- high wind speeds

50

USDA Forest Service Gen. Tech. Rep. RMRS-GTR-192. 2007

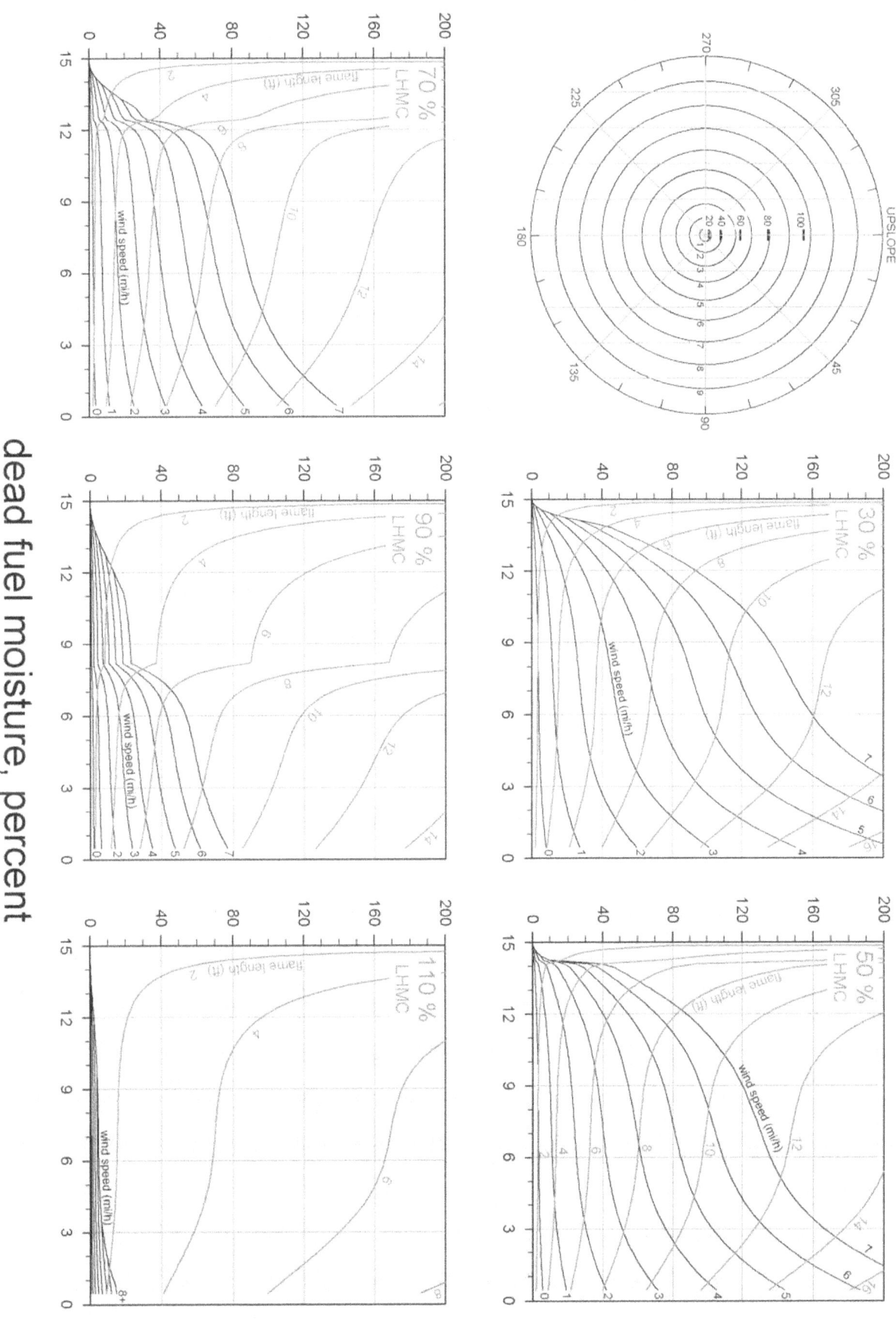

rate of spread, ch/h

dead fuel moisture, percent

GR4 (104)- low wind speeds

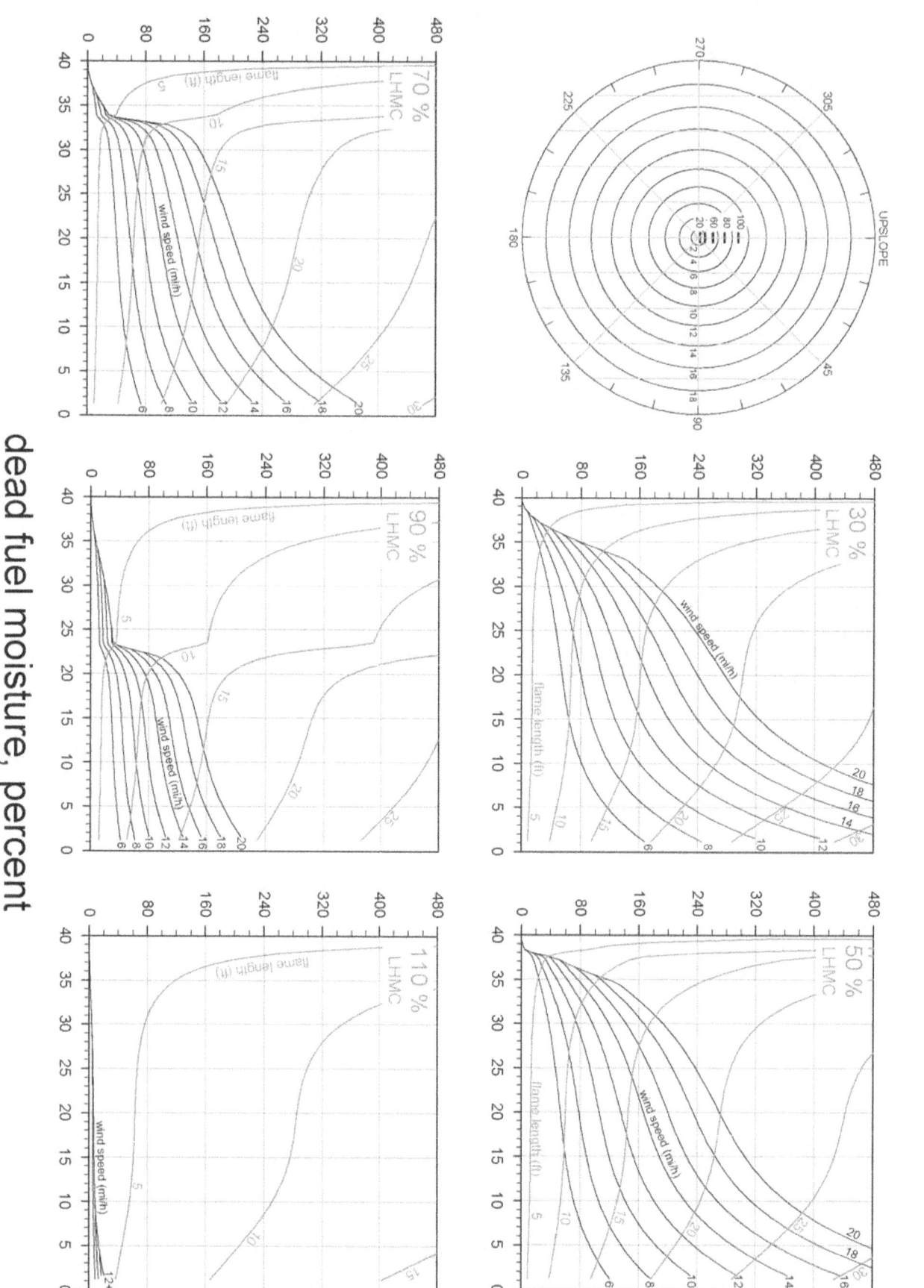

rate of spread, ch/h

dead fuel moisture, percent

GR5 (105)- high wind speeds

USDA Forest Service Gen. Tech. Rep. RMRS-GTR-192. 2007

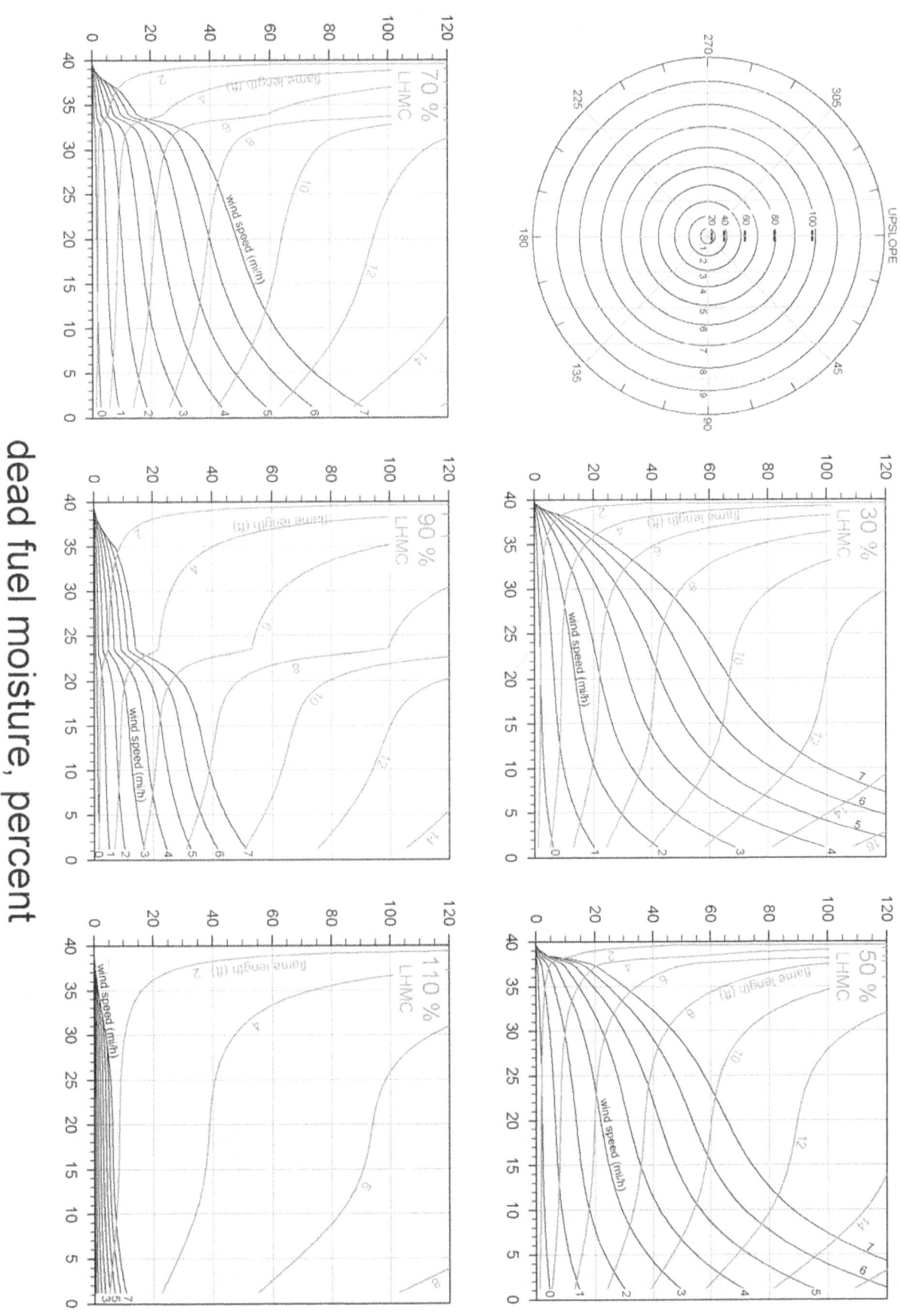

rate of spread, ch/h

dead fuel moisture, percent

GR5 (105)- low wind speeds

USDA Forest Service Gen. Tech. Rep. RMRS-GTR-192. 2007

53

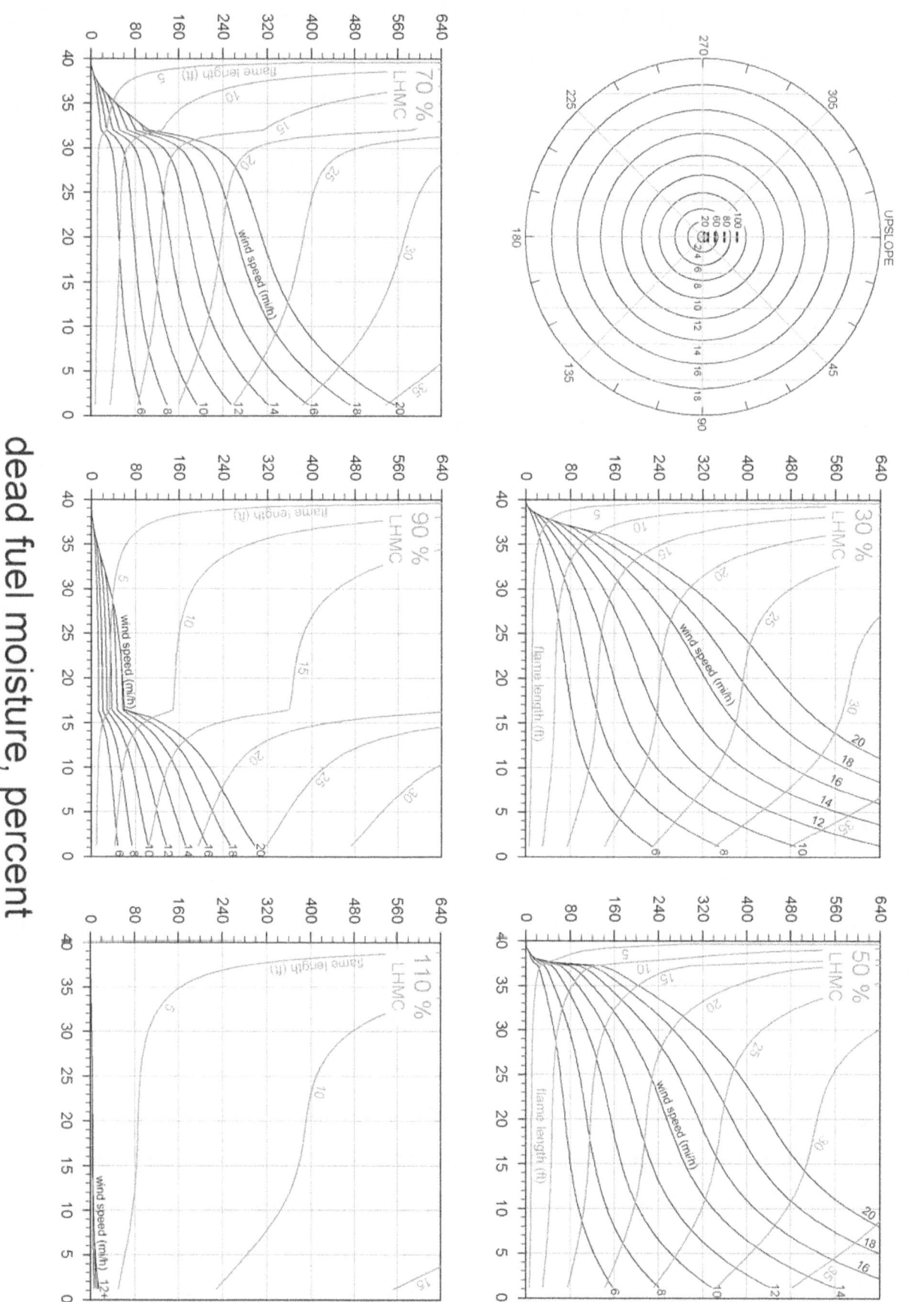

rate of spread, ch/h

dead fuel moisture, percent

GR6 (106)- high wind speeds

54

USDA Forest Service Gen. Tech. Rep. RMRS-GTR-192. 2007

rate of spread, ch/h

GR6 (106)- low wind speeds

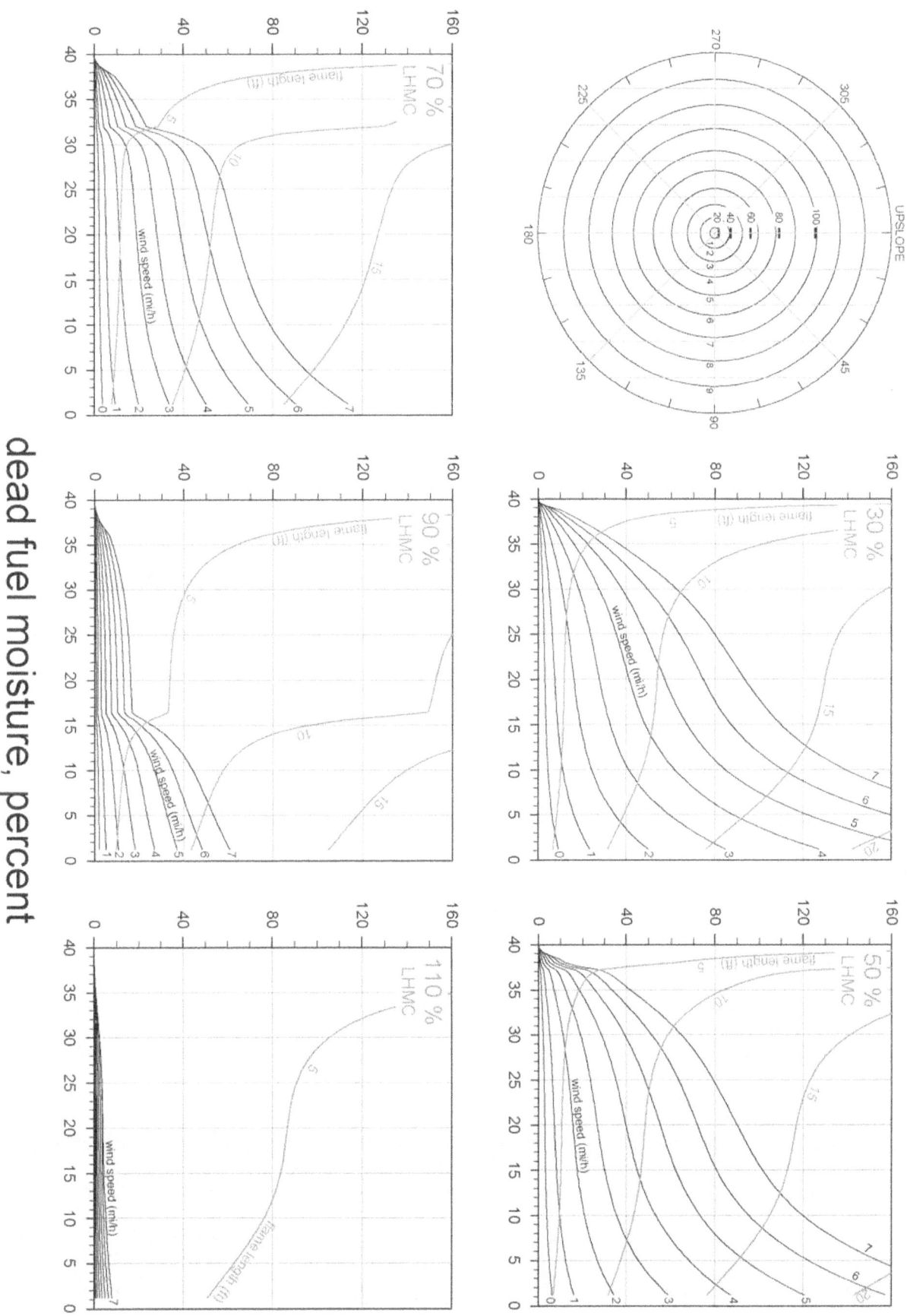

dead fuel moisture, percent

USDA Forest Service Gen. Tech. Rep. RMRS-GTR-192. 2007

55

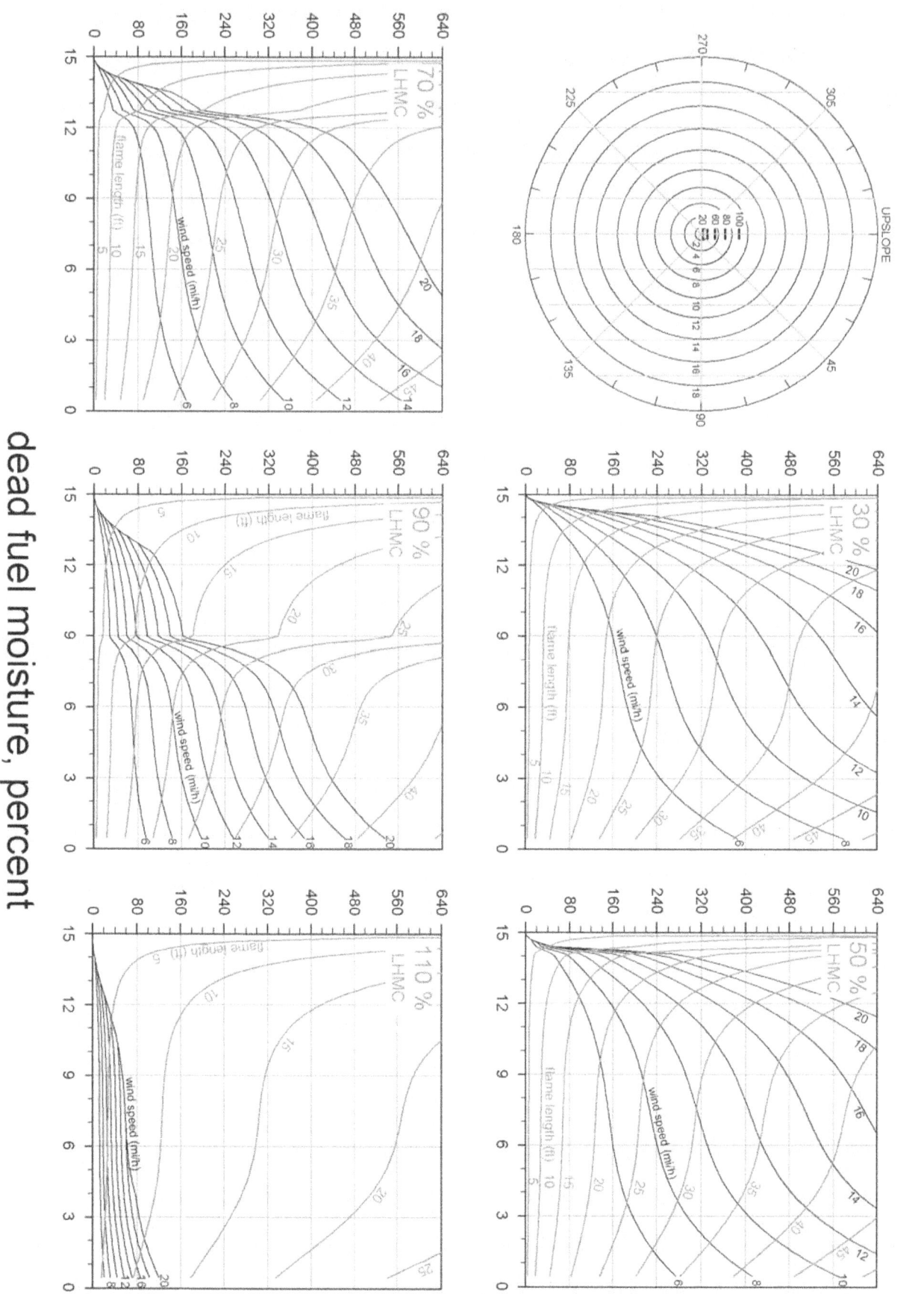

rate of spread, ch/h

dead fuel moisture, percent

GR7 (107)- high wind speeds

USDA Forest Service Gen. Tech. Rep. RMRS-GTR-192. 2007

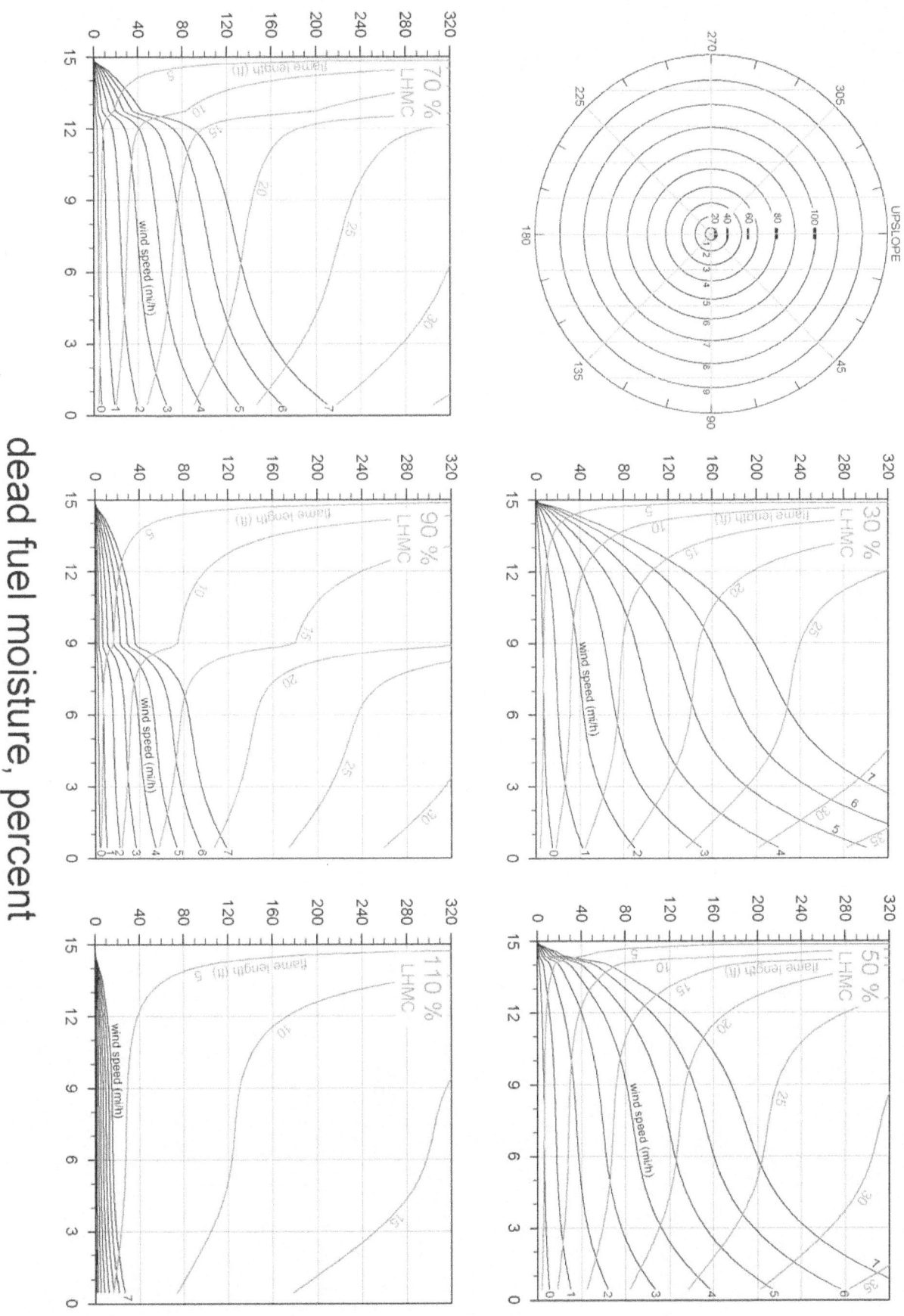

rate of spread, ch/h

dead fuel moisture, percent

GR7 (107)- low wind speeds

USDA Forest Service Gen. Tech. Rep. RMRS-GTR-192. 2007

57

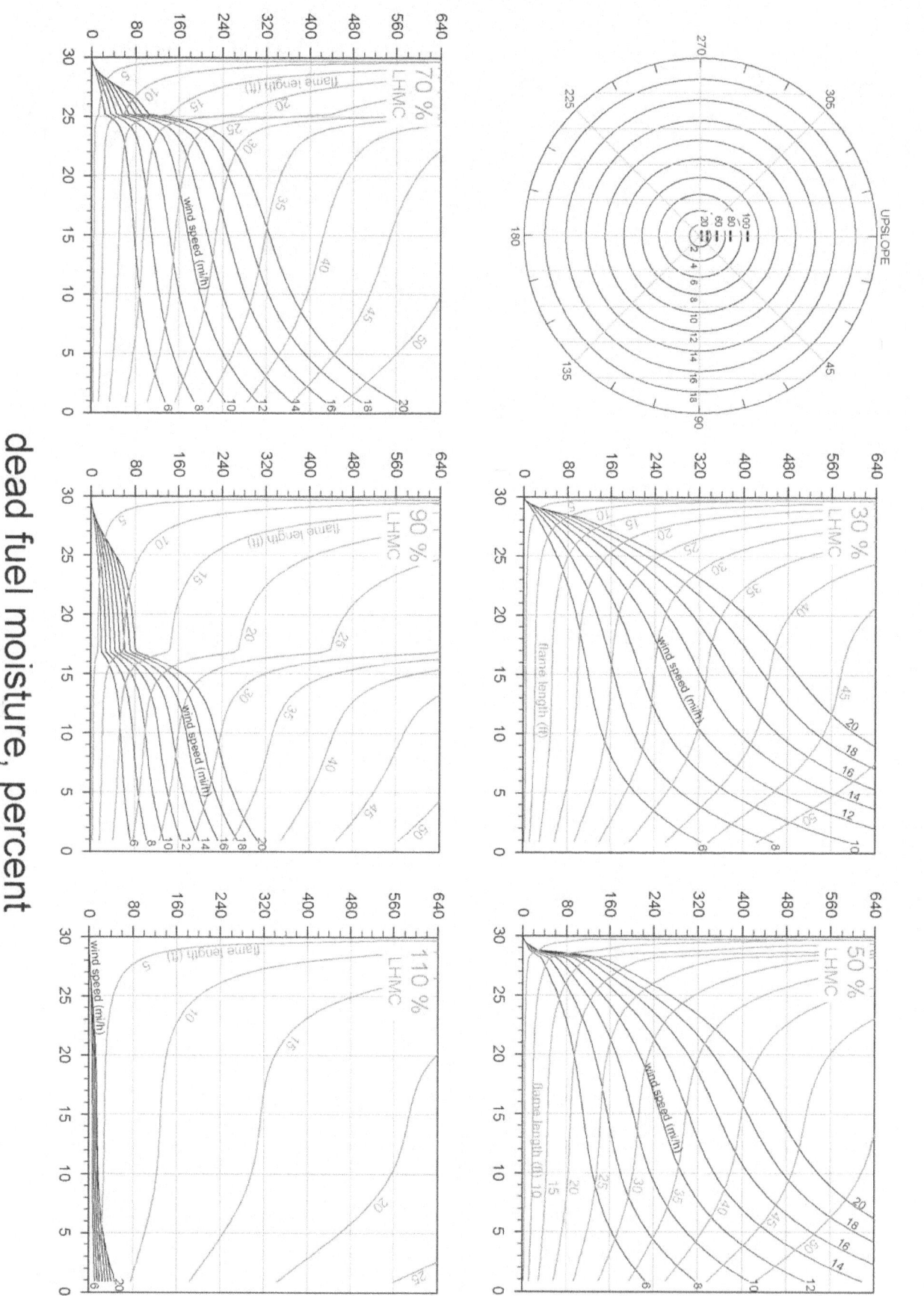

rate of spread, ch/h

dead fuel moisture, percent

GR8 (108)- high wind speeds

USDA Forest Service Gen. Tech. Rep. RMRS-GTR-192. 2007

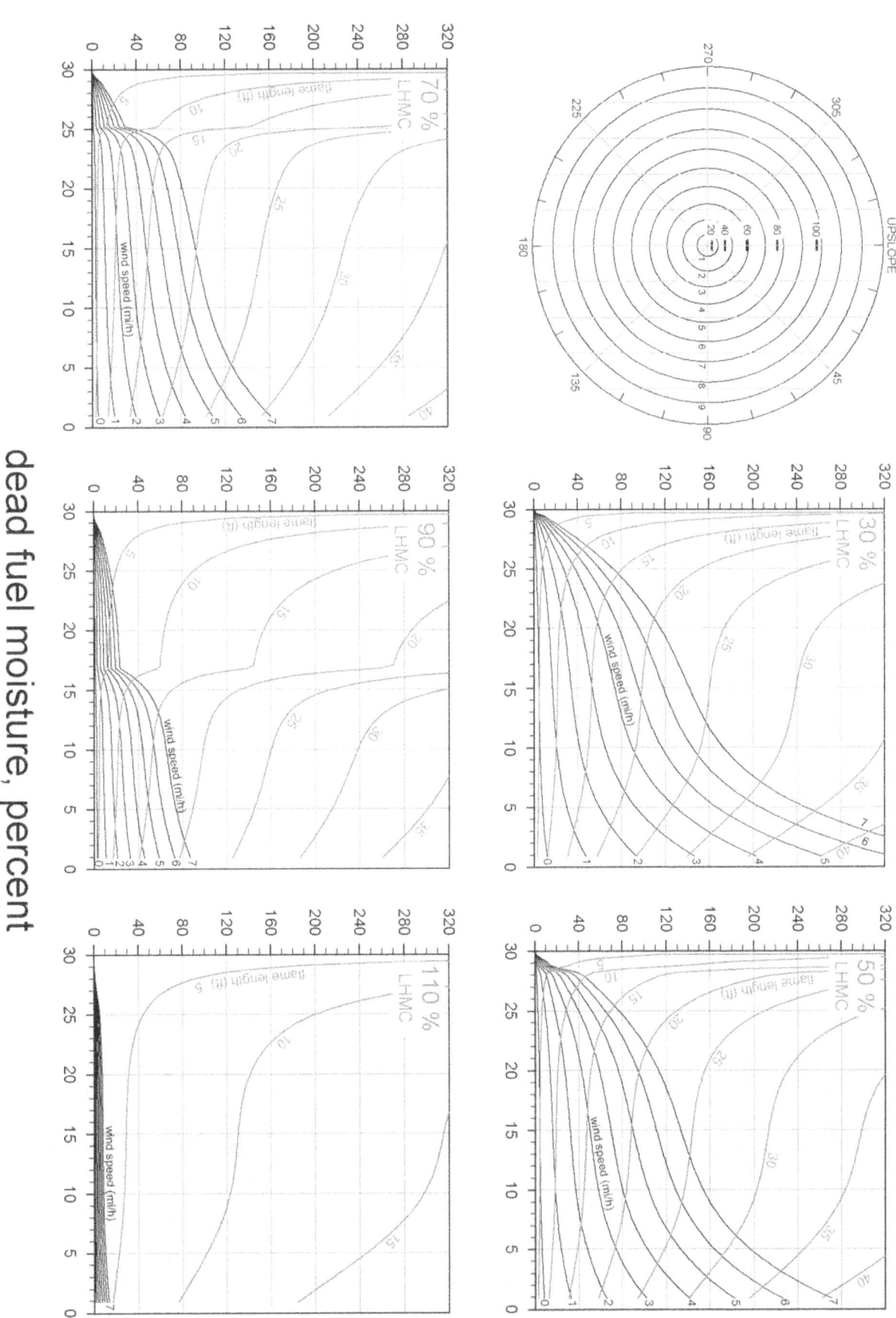

rate of spread, ch/h

dead fuel moisture, percent

GR8 (108)- low wind speeds

USDA Forest Service Gen. Tech. Rep. RMRS-GTR-192. 2007

59

rate of spread, ch/h

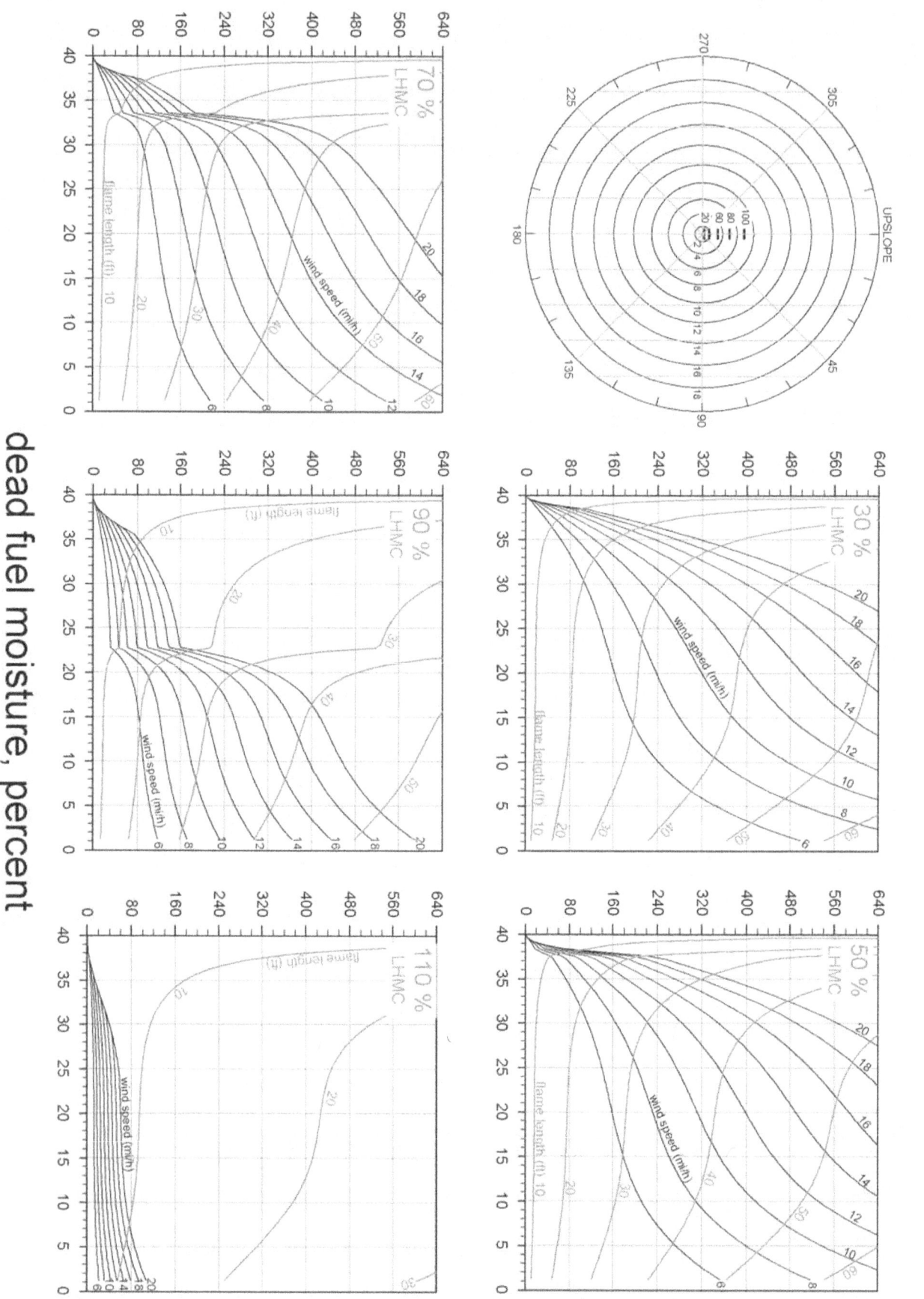

GR9 (109)- high wind speeds

dead fuel moisture, percent

USDA Forest Service Gen. Tech. Rep. RMRS-GTR-192. 2007

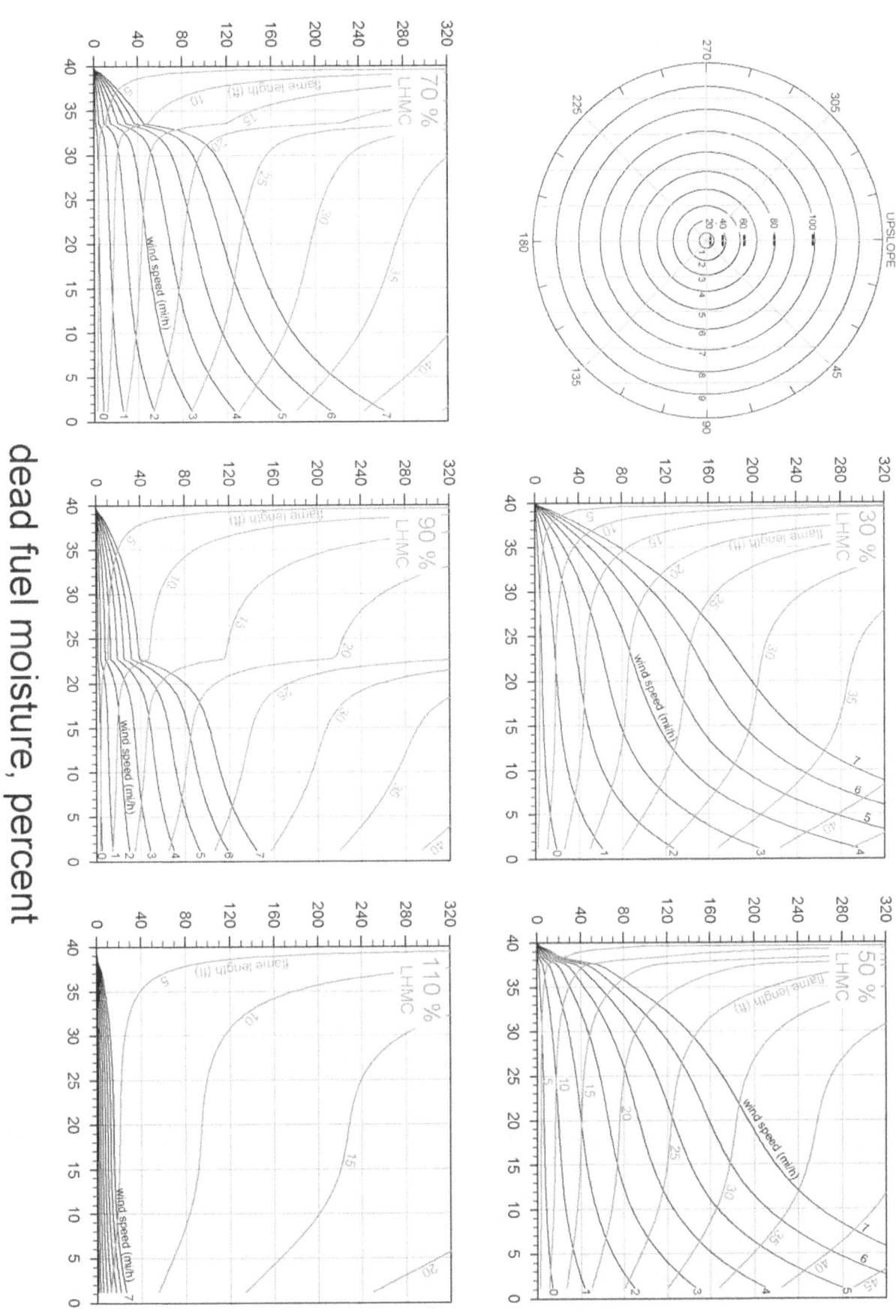

rate of spread, ch/h

dead fuel moisture, percent

GR9 (109)- low wind speeds

USDA Forest Service Gen. Tech. Rep. RMRS-GTR-192. 2007

61

62

USDA Forest Service Gen. Tech. Rep. RMRS-GTR-192. 2007

Grass-shrub

USDA Forest Service Gen. Tech. Rep. RMRS-GTR-192. 2007

63

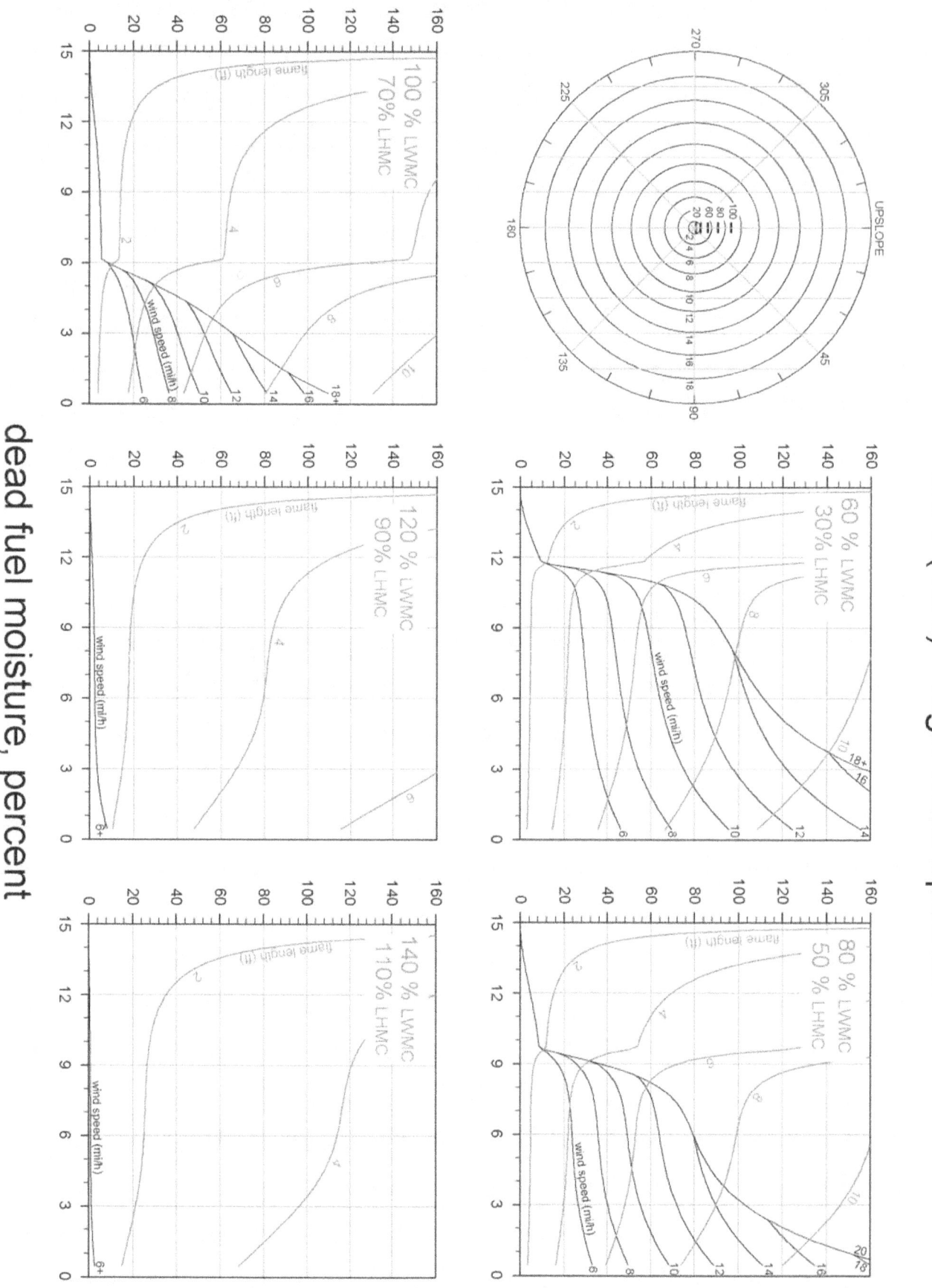

rate of spread, ch/h

dead fuel moisture, percent

GS1 (121) - high wind speeds

64

USDA Forest Service Gen. Tech. Rep. RMRS-GTR-192. 2007

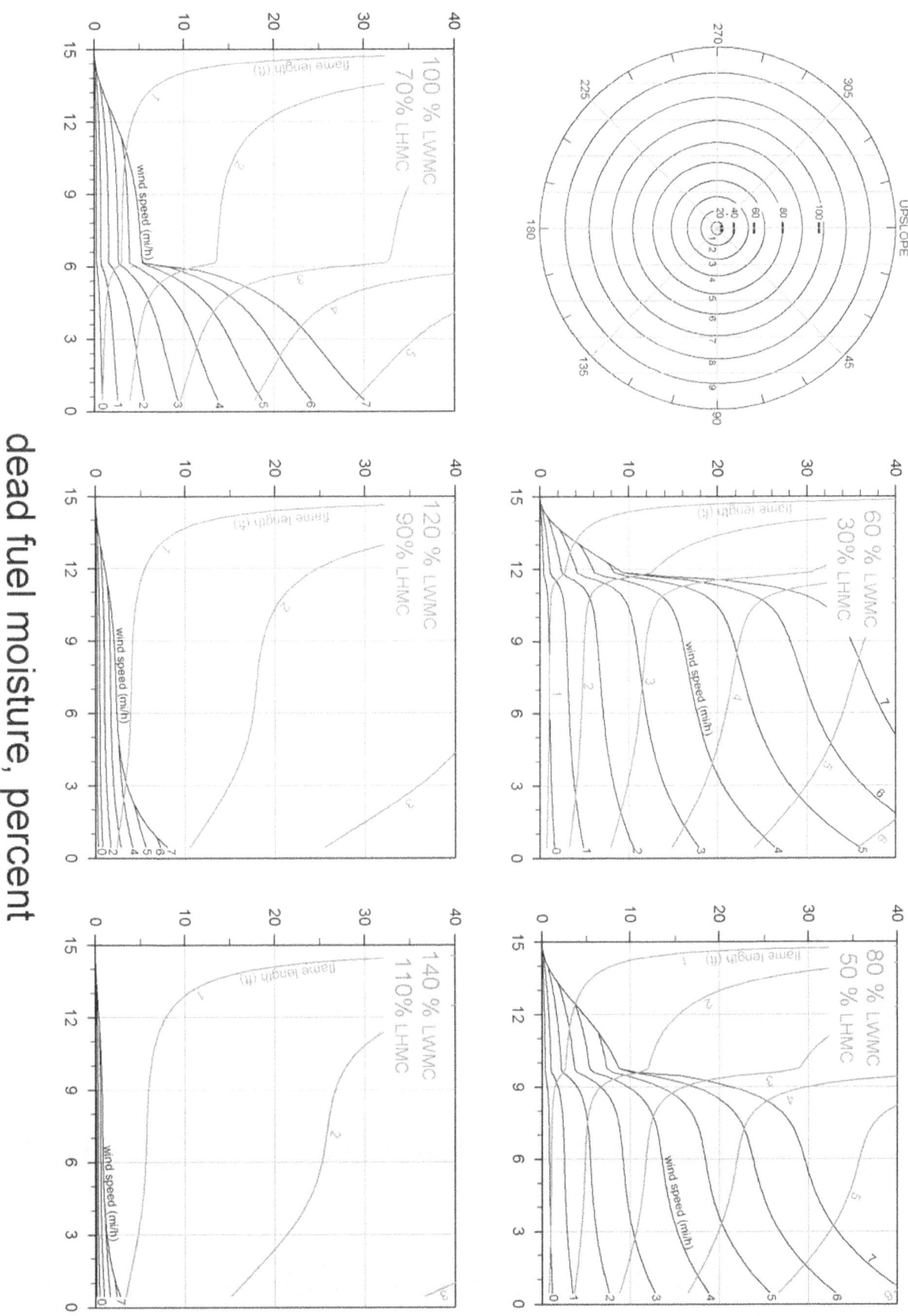

rate of spread, ch/h

dead fuel moisture, percent

GS1 (121) - low wind speeds

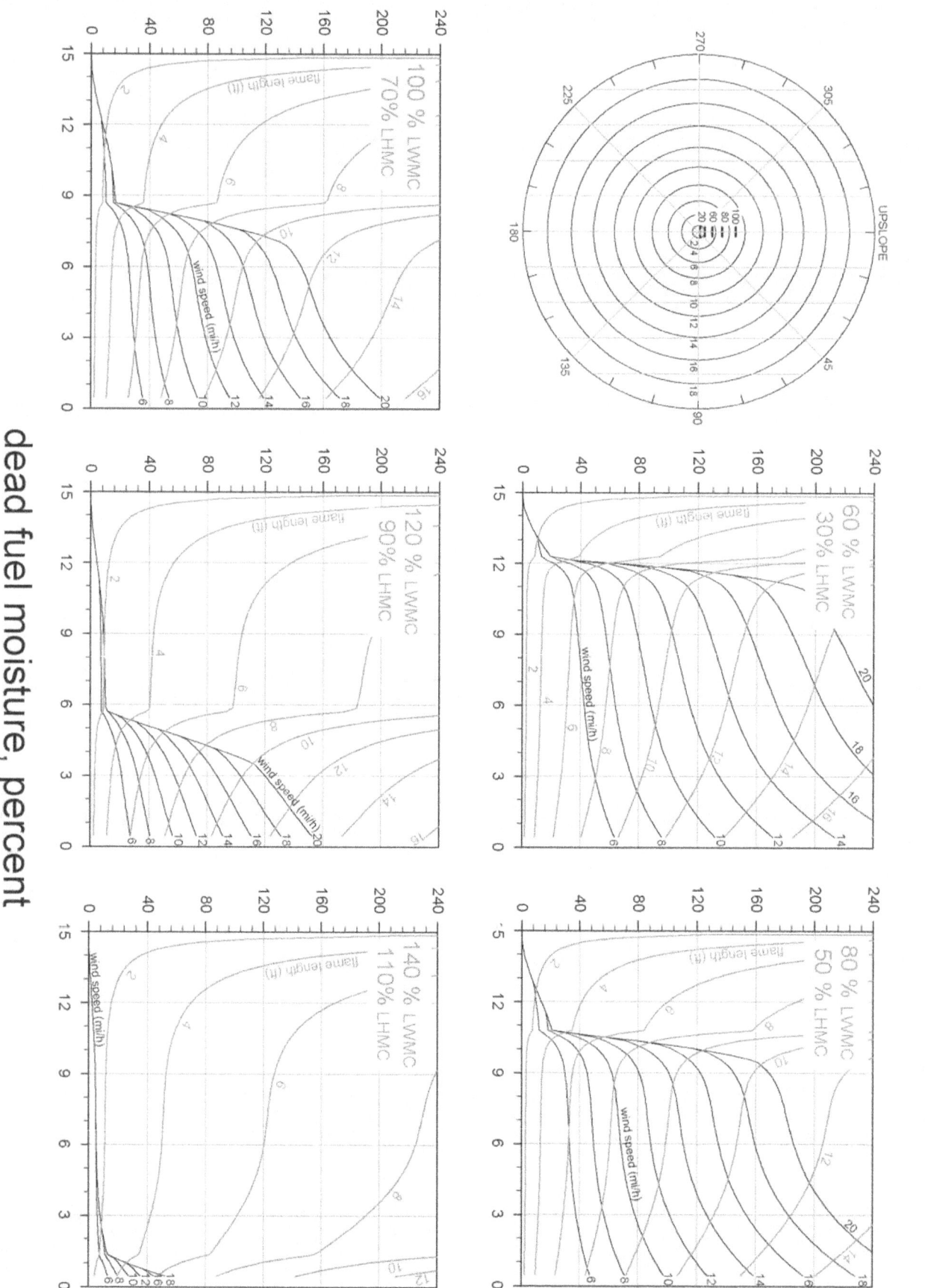

rate of spread, ch/h

dead fuel moisture, percent

GS2 (122) - high wind speeds

USDA Forest Service Gen. Tech. Rep. RMRS-GTR-192. 2007

rate of spread, ch/h

GS2 (122) - low wind speeds

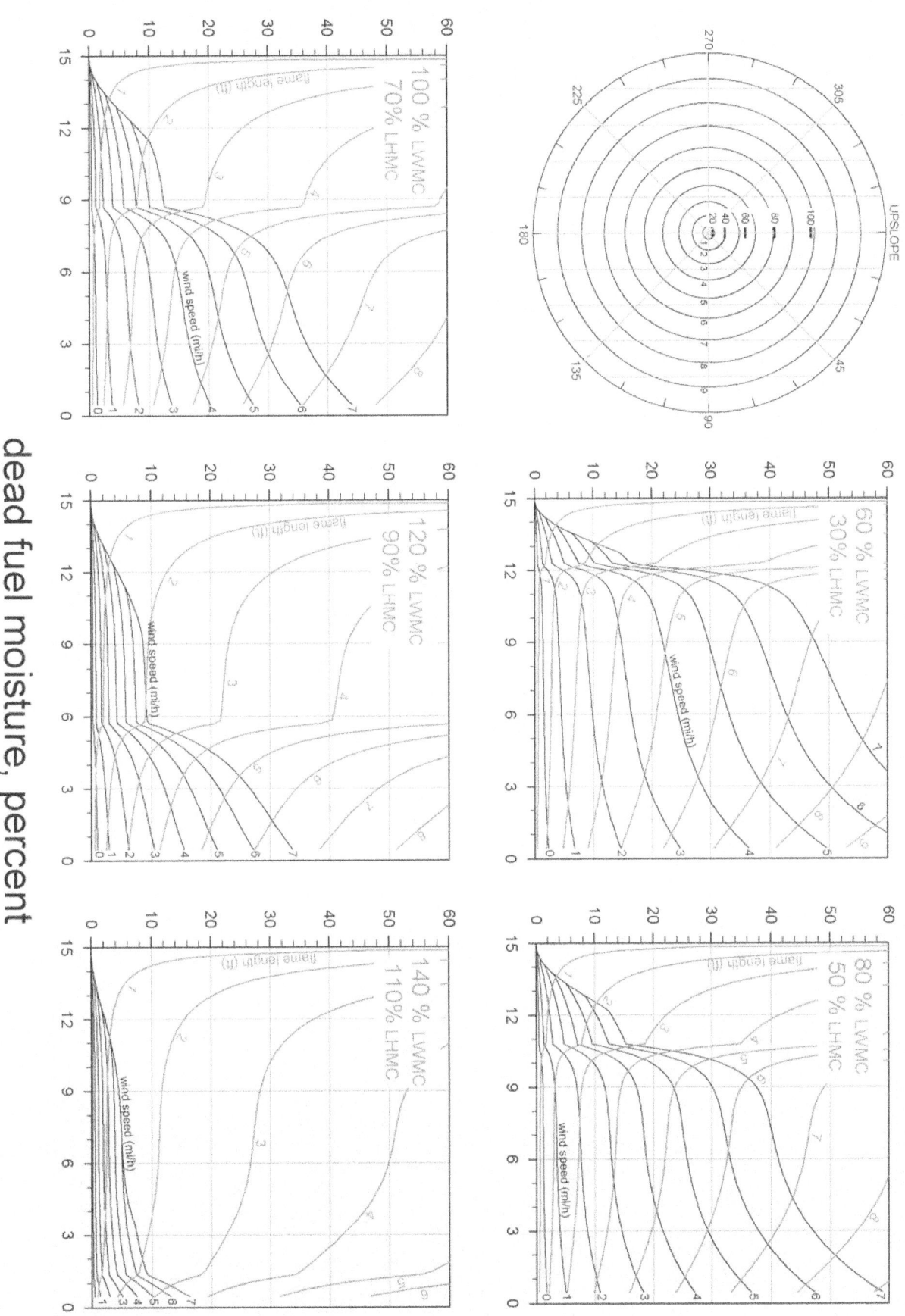

dead fuel moisture, percent

USDA Forest Service Gen. Tech. Rep. RMRS-GTR-192. 2007

67

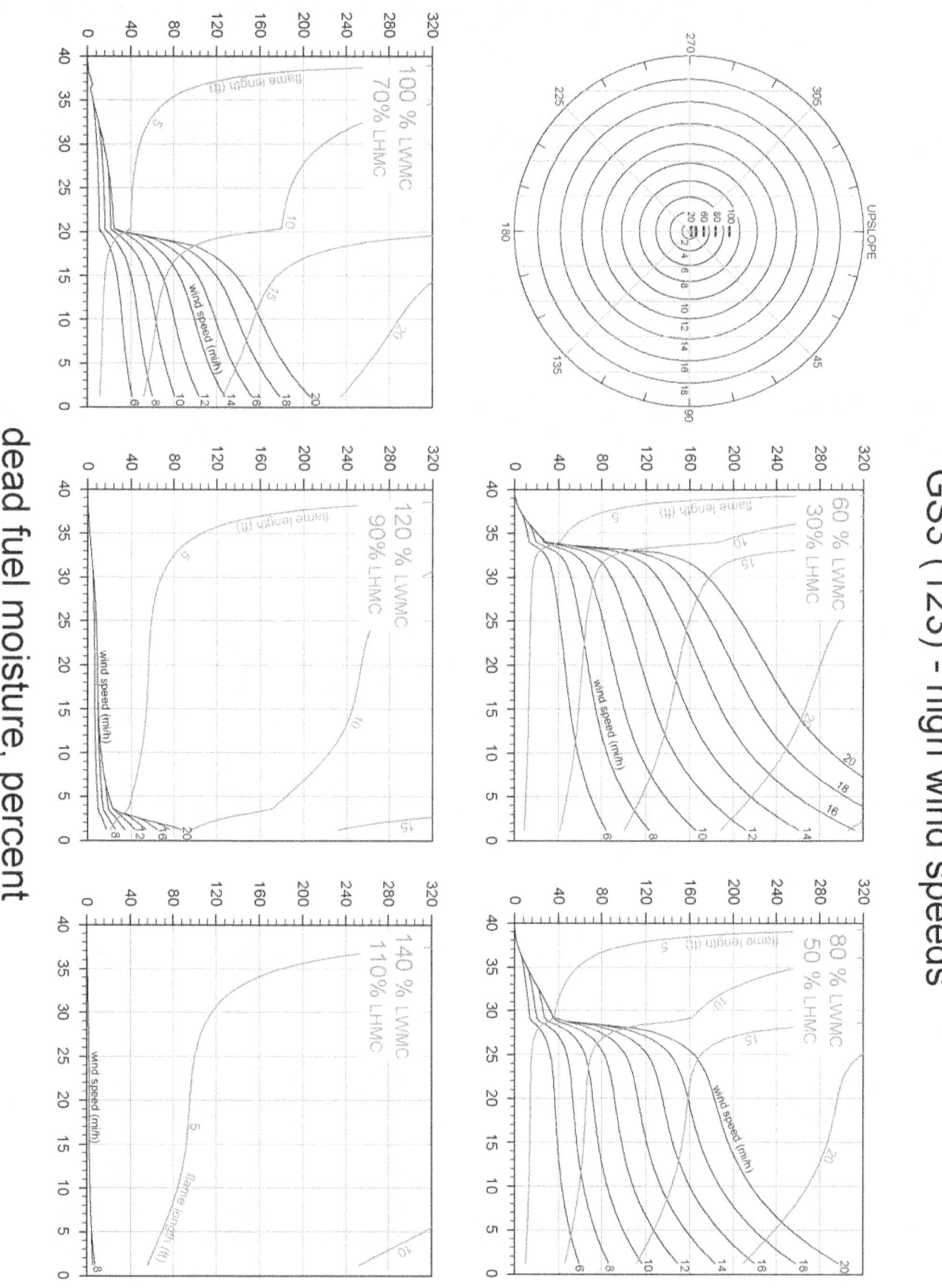

rate of spread, ch/h

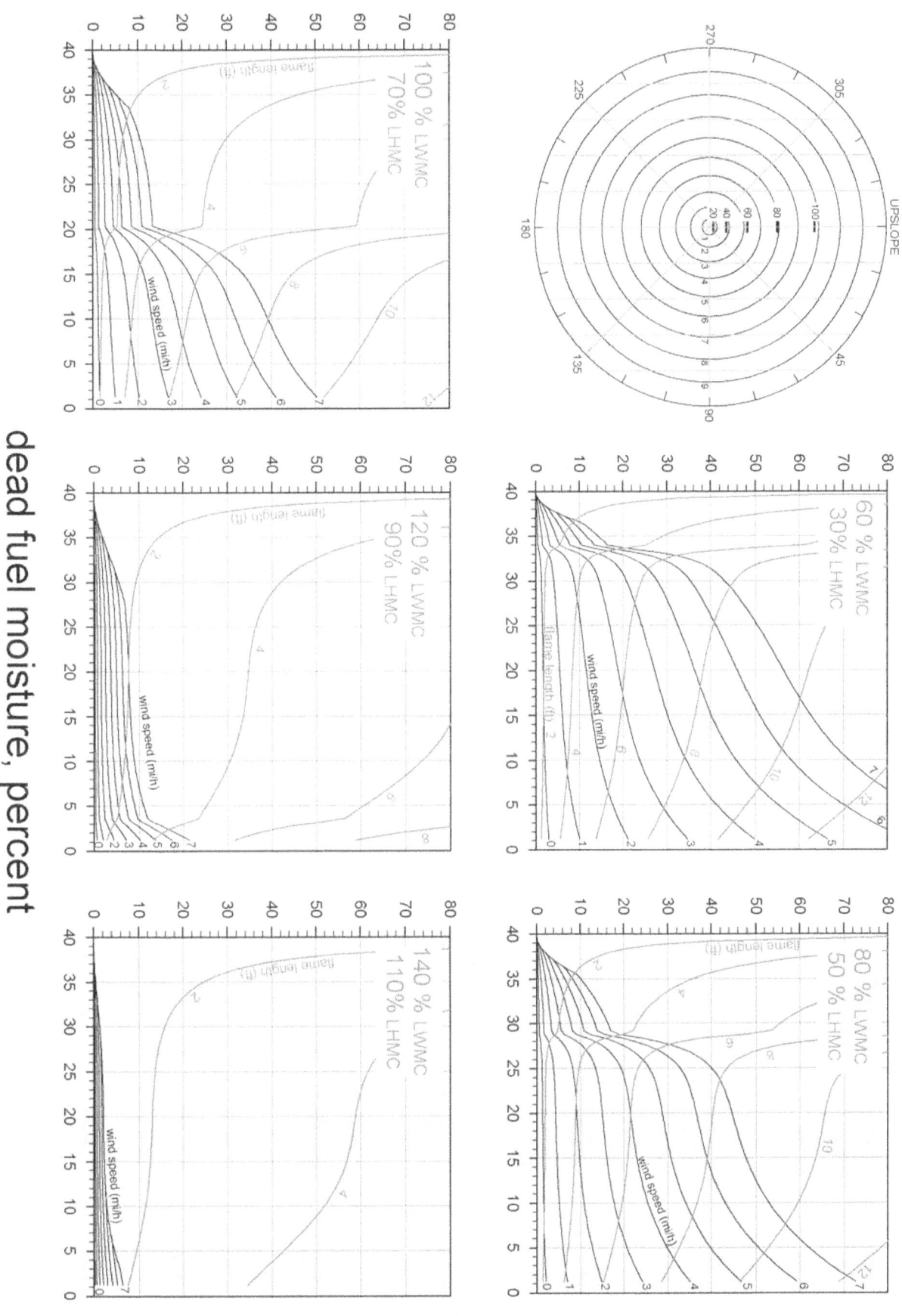

GS3 (123) - low wind speeds

dead fuel moisture, percent

100 % LWMC
70% LHMC

120 % LWMC
90% LHMC

140 % LWMC
110% LHMC

60 % LWMC
30% LHMC

80 % LWMC
50% LHMC

flame length (ft)

wind speed (mi/h)

UPSLOPE

USDA Forest Service Gen. Tech. Rep. RMRS-GTR-192. 2007

69

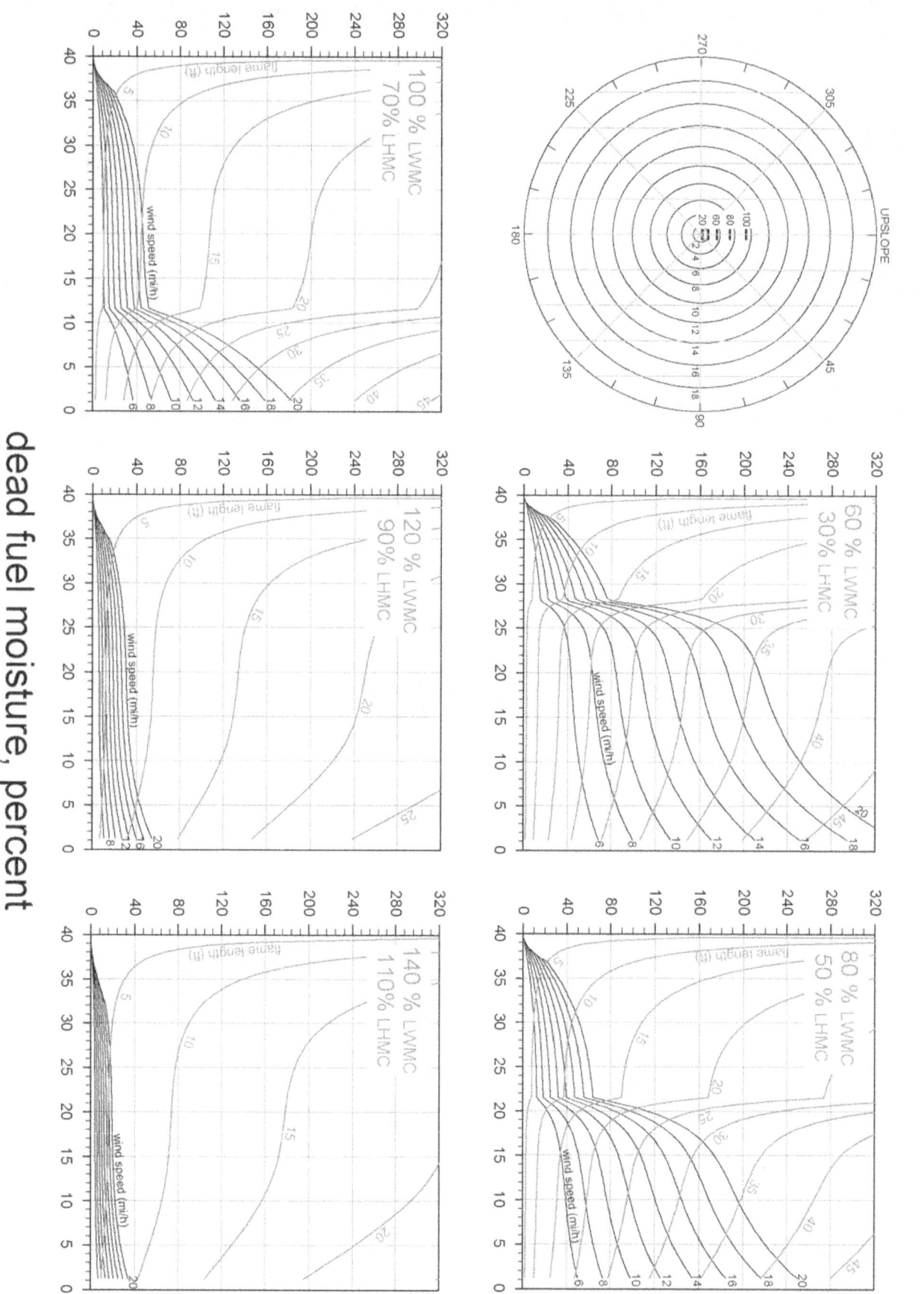

rate of spread, ch/h

dead fuel moisture, percent

GS4 (124) - high wind speeds

USDA Forest Service Gen. Tech. Rep. RMRS-GTR-192. 2007

rate of spread, ch/h

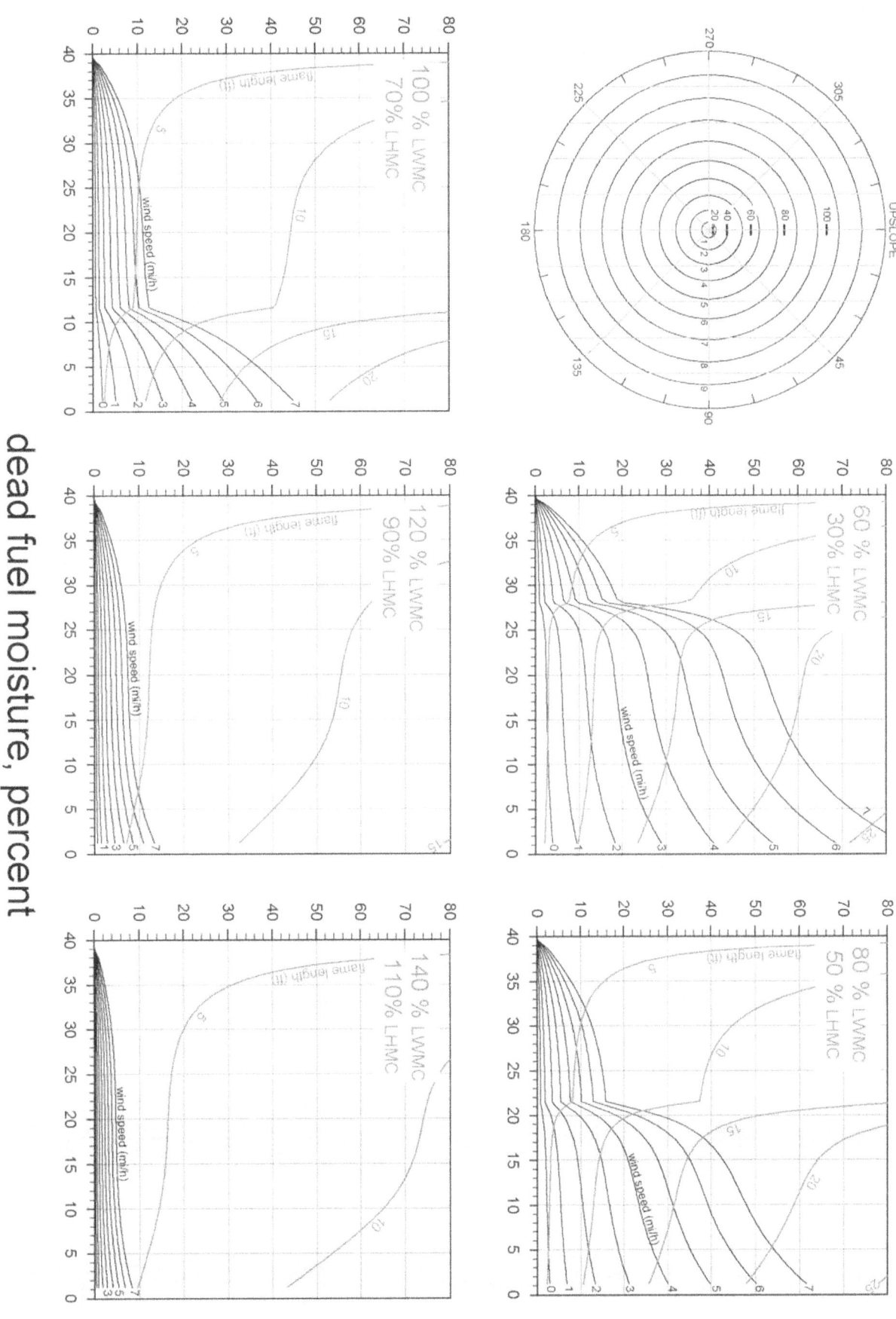

GS4 (124) - low wind speeds

USDA Forest Service Gen. Tech. Rep. RMRS-GTR-192. 2007

71

Shrub

USDA Forest Service Gen. Tech. Rep. RMRS-GTR-192. 2007

73

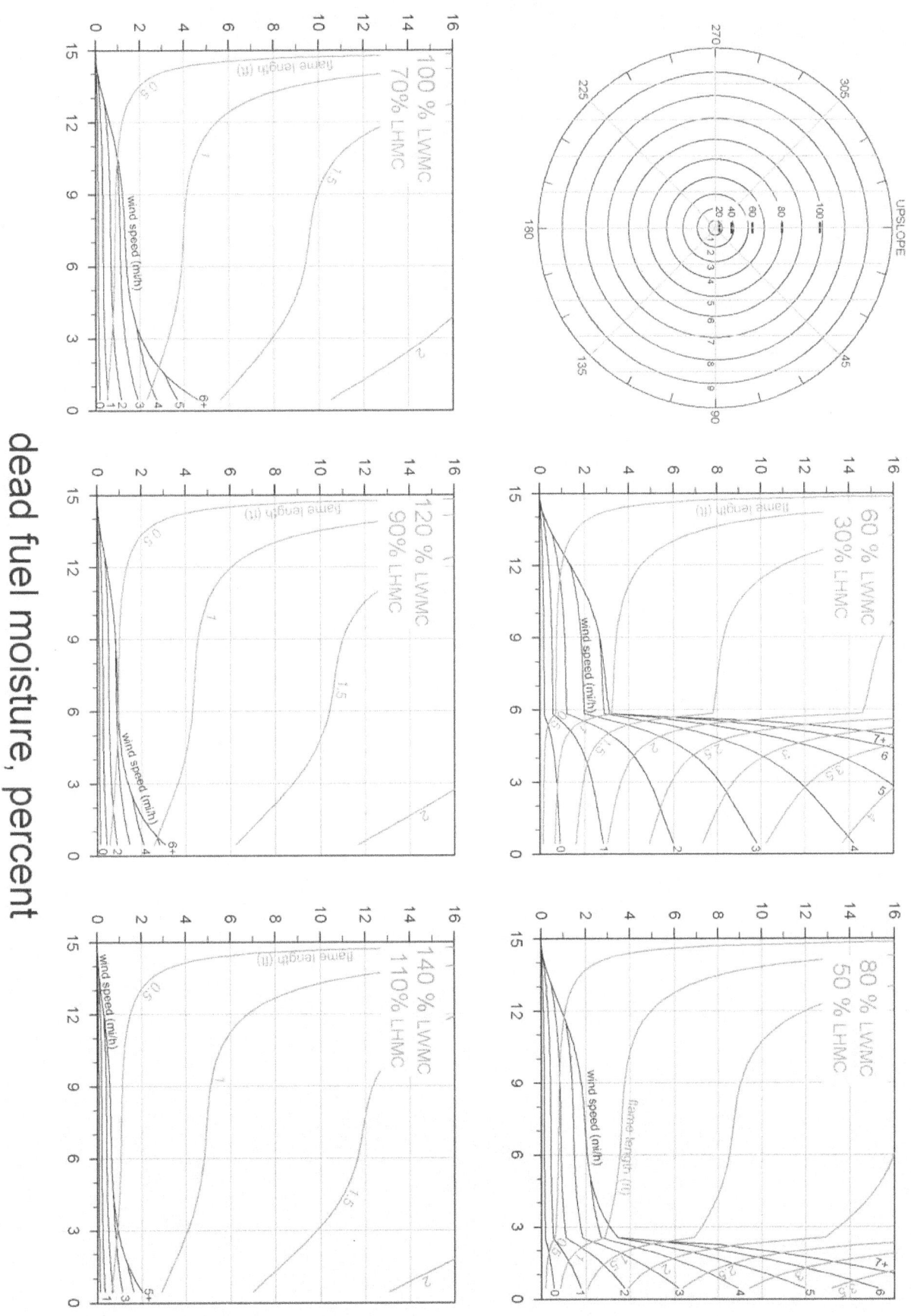

USDA Forest Service Gen. Tech. Rep. RMRS-GTR-192. 2007

75

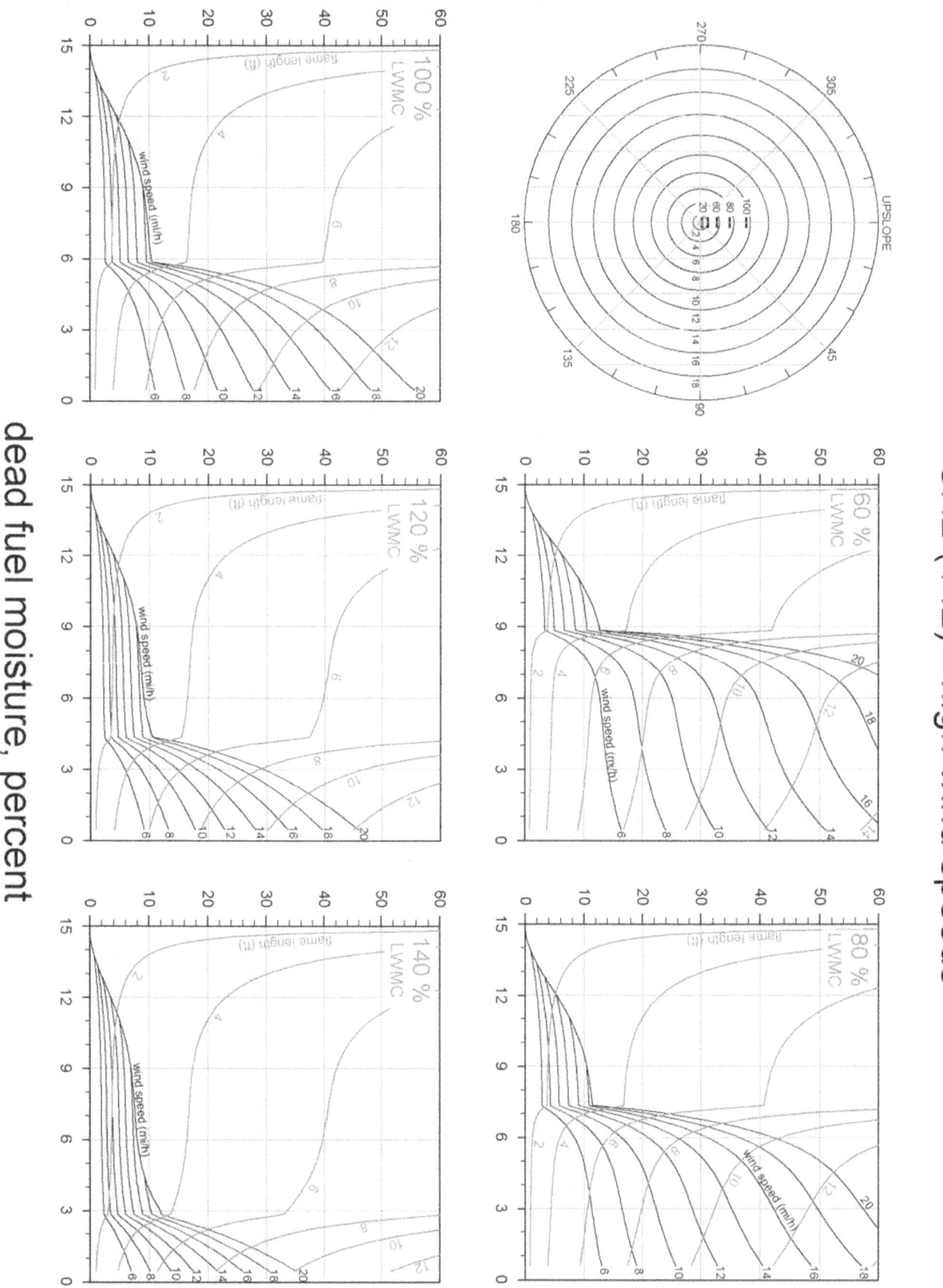

SH2 (142) - high wind speeds

rate of spread, ch/h

dead fuel moisture, percent

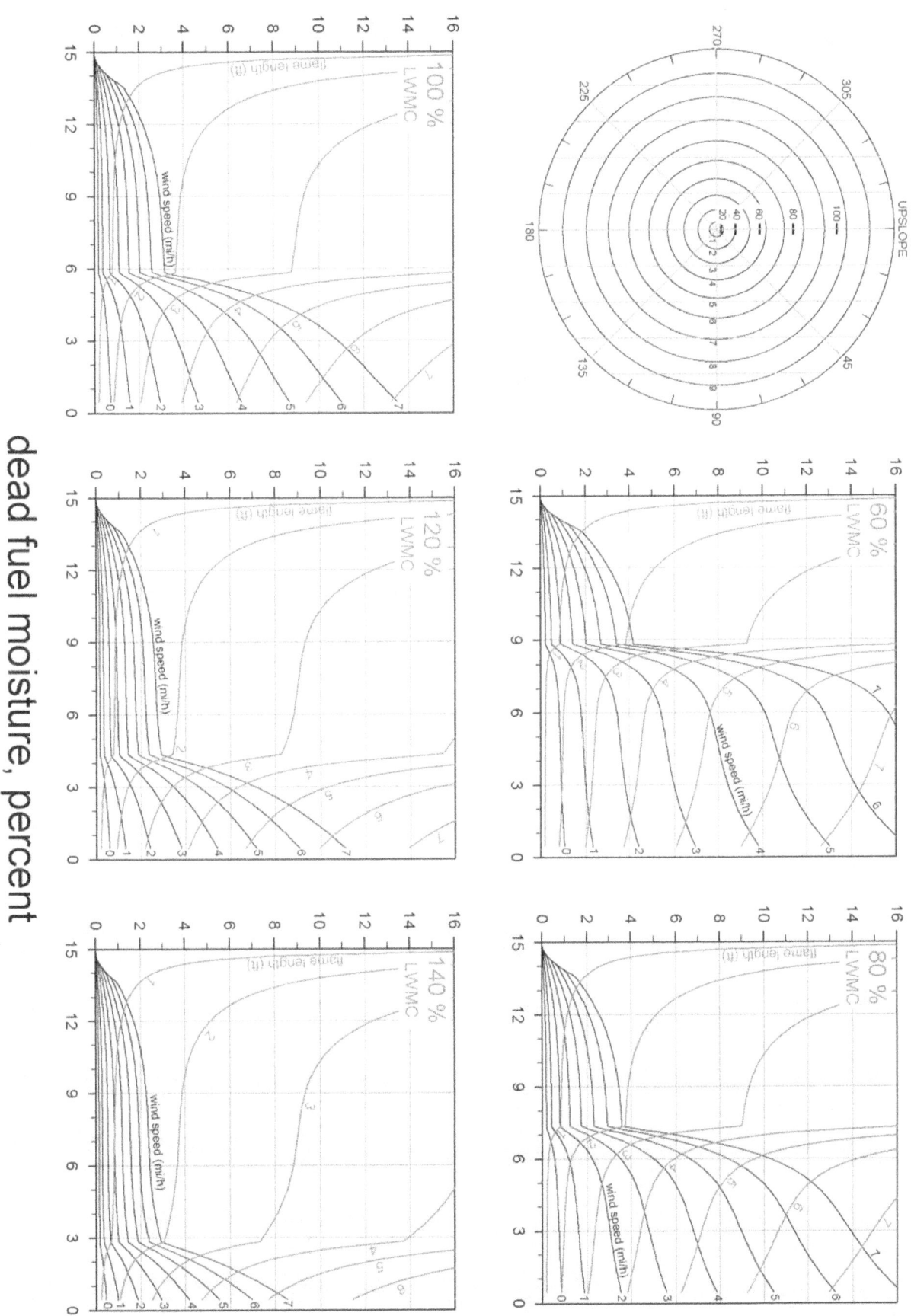

SH2 (142) - low wind speeds

rate of spread, ch/h

dead fuel moisture, percent

USDA Forest Service Gen. Tech. Rep. RMRS-GTR-192. 2007

77

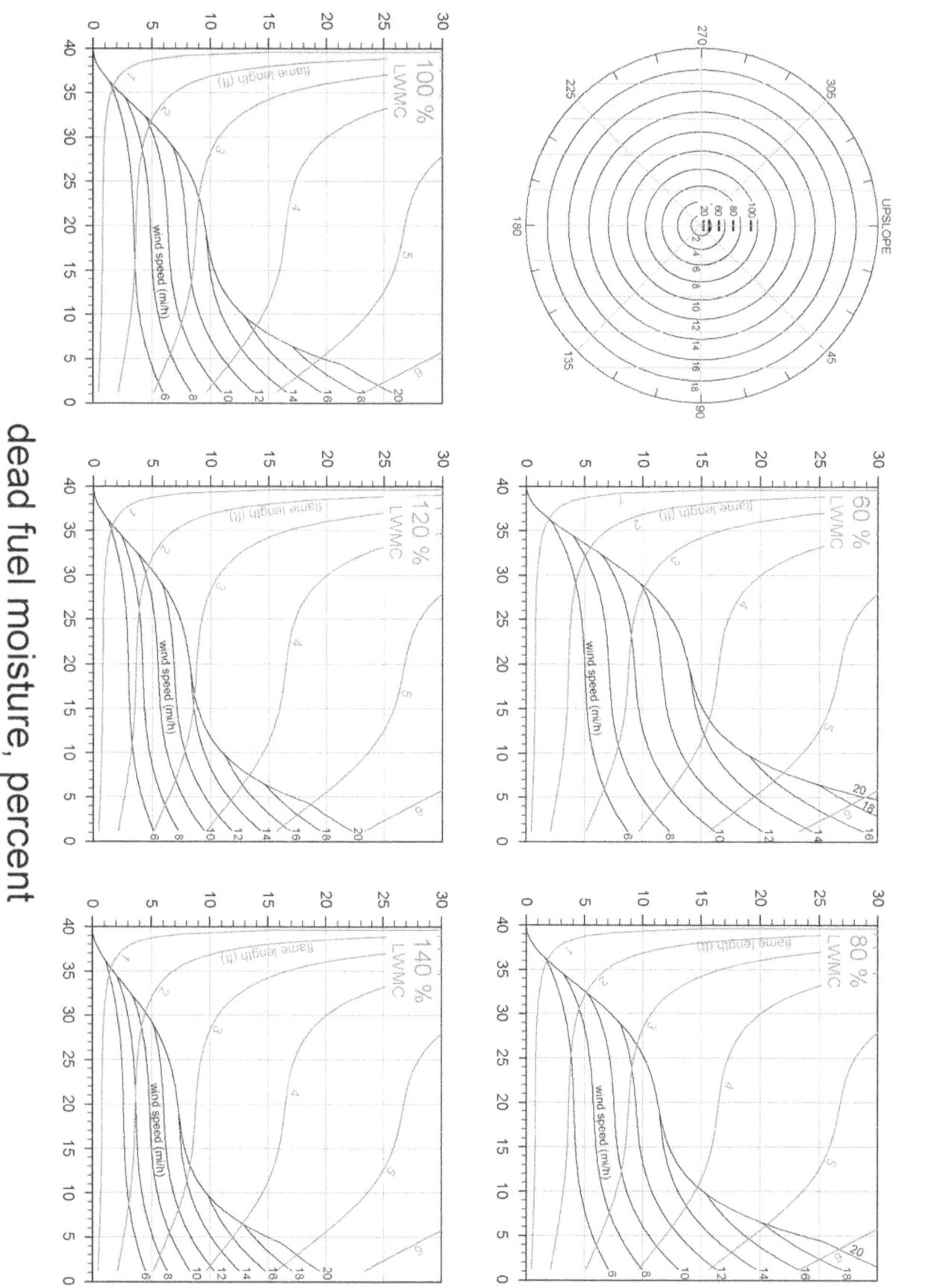

rate of spread, ch/h

dead fuel moisture, percent

SH3 (143) - high wind speeds

USDA Forest Service Gen. Tech. Rep. RMRS-GTR-192. 2007

rate of spread, ch/h

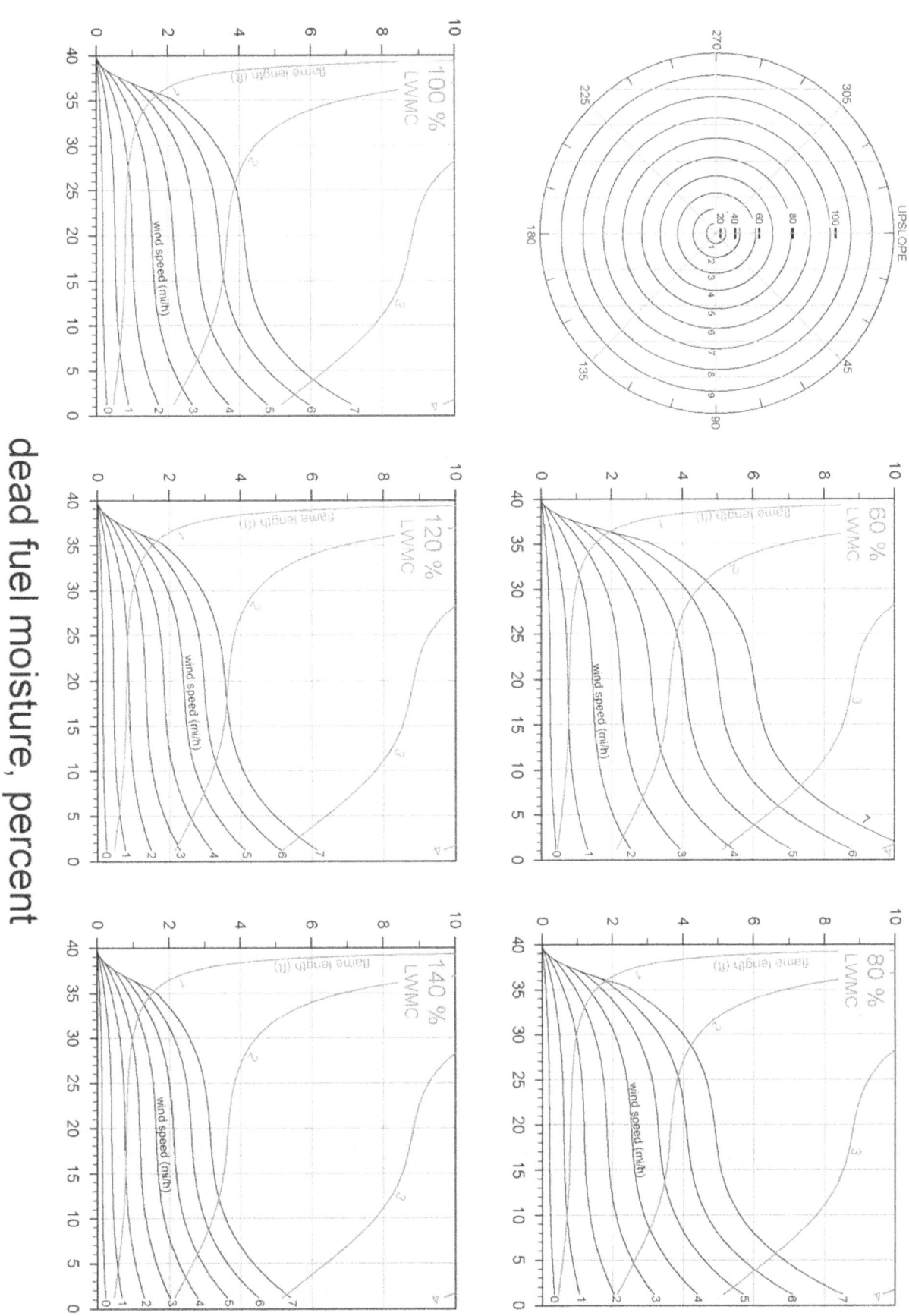

SH3 (143) - low wind speeds

dead fuel moisture, percent

USDA Forest Service Gen. Tech. Rep. RMRS-GTR-192. 2007

79

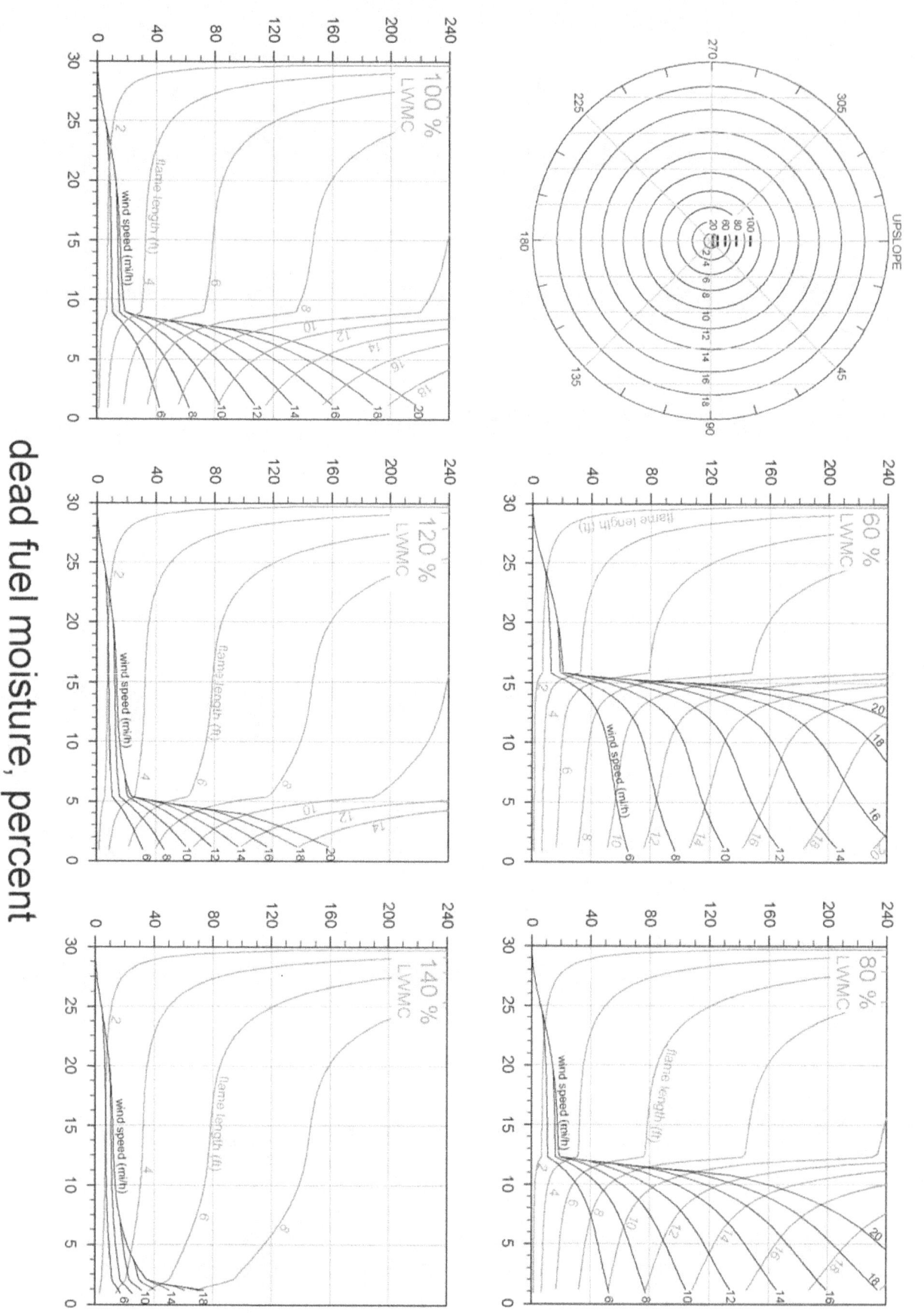

rate of spread, ch/h

dead fuel moisture, percent

SH4 (144)- high wind speeds

100 %
LWMC

120 %
LWMC

140 %
LWMC

60 %
LWMC

80 %
LWMC

UPSLOPE

80

rate of spread, ch/h

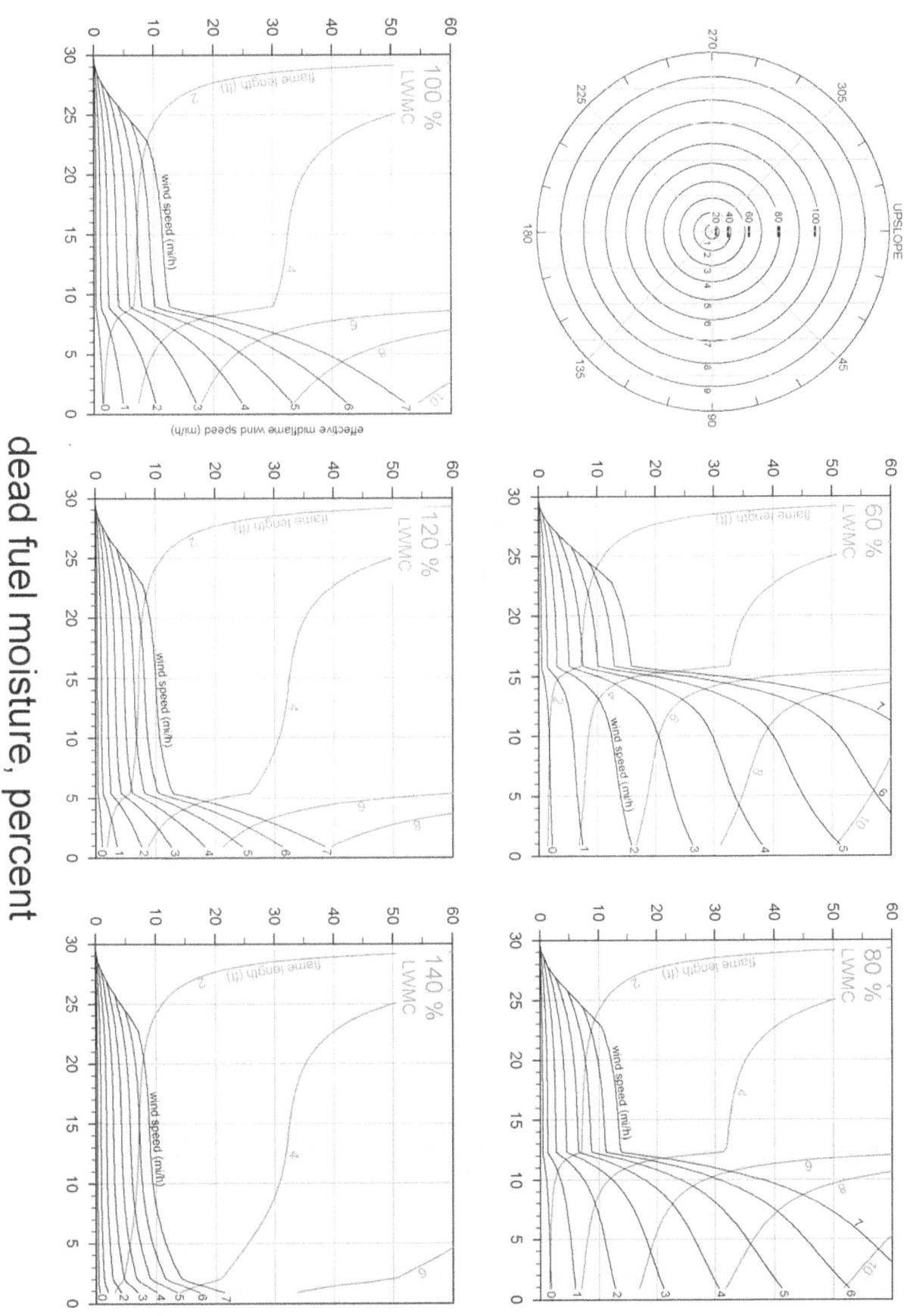

dead fuel moisture, percent

SH4 (144)- low wind speeds

USDA Forest Service Gen. Tech. Rep. RMRS-GTR-192. 2007

81

rate of spread, ch/h

dead fuel moisture, percent

SH5 (145)- high wind speeds

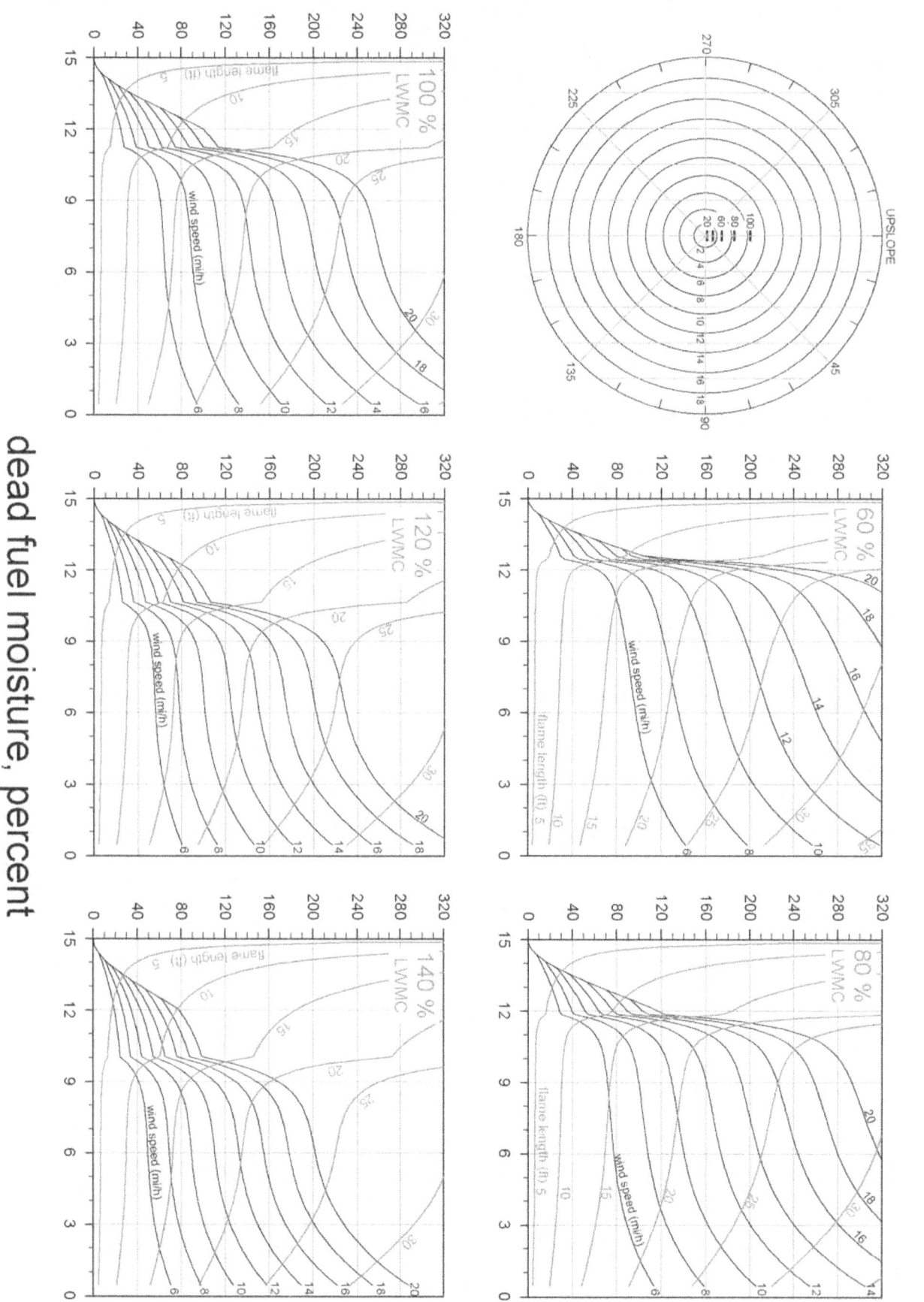

USDA Forest Service Gen. Tech. Rep. RMRS-GTR-192. 2007

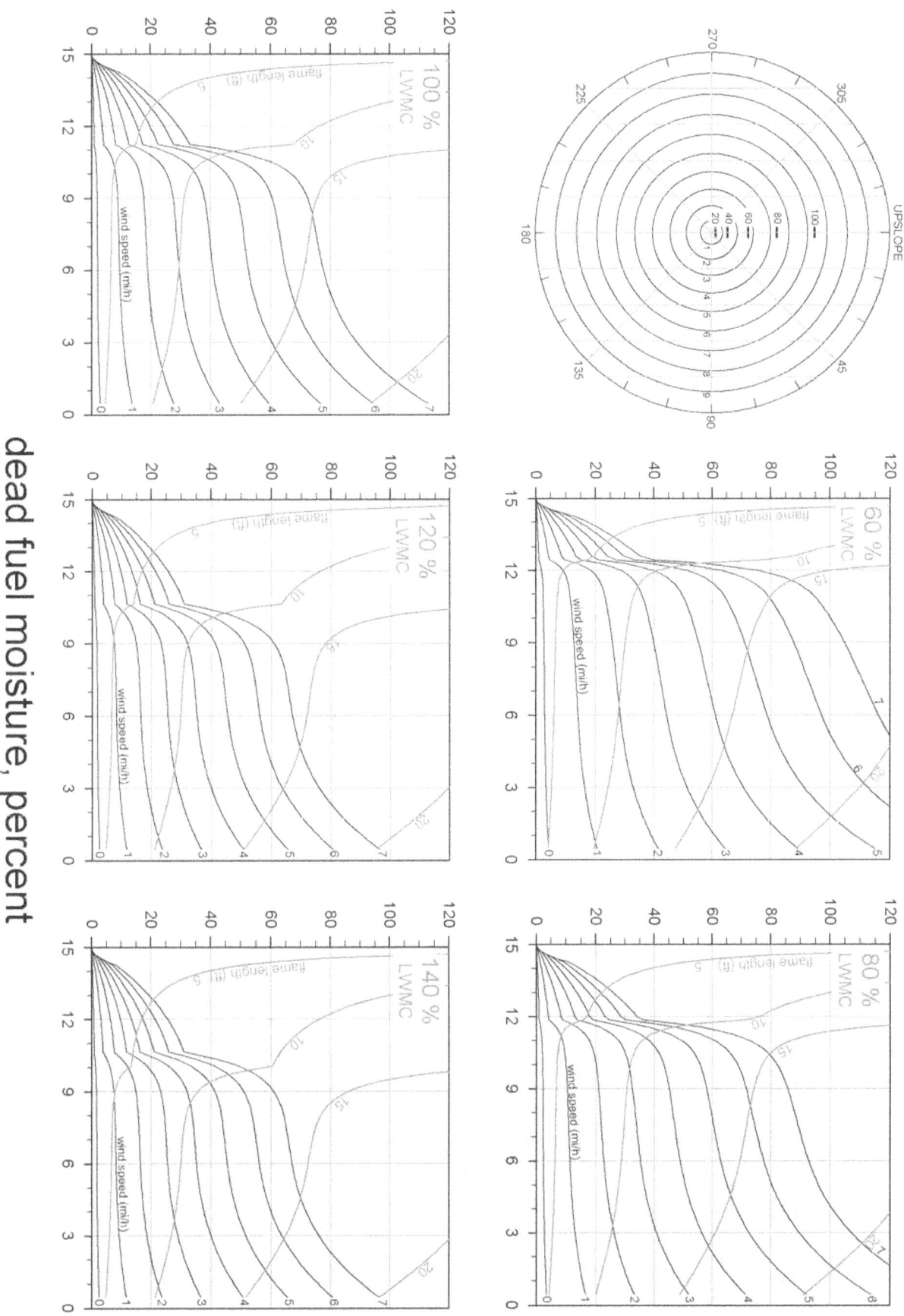

rate of spread, ch/h

SH5 (145)- low wind speeds

dead fuel moisture, percent

USDA Forest Service Gen. Tech. Rep. RMRS-GTR-192. 2007

83

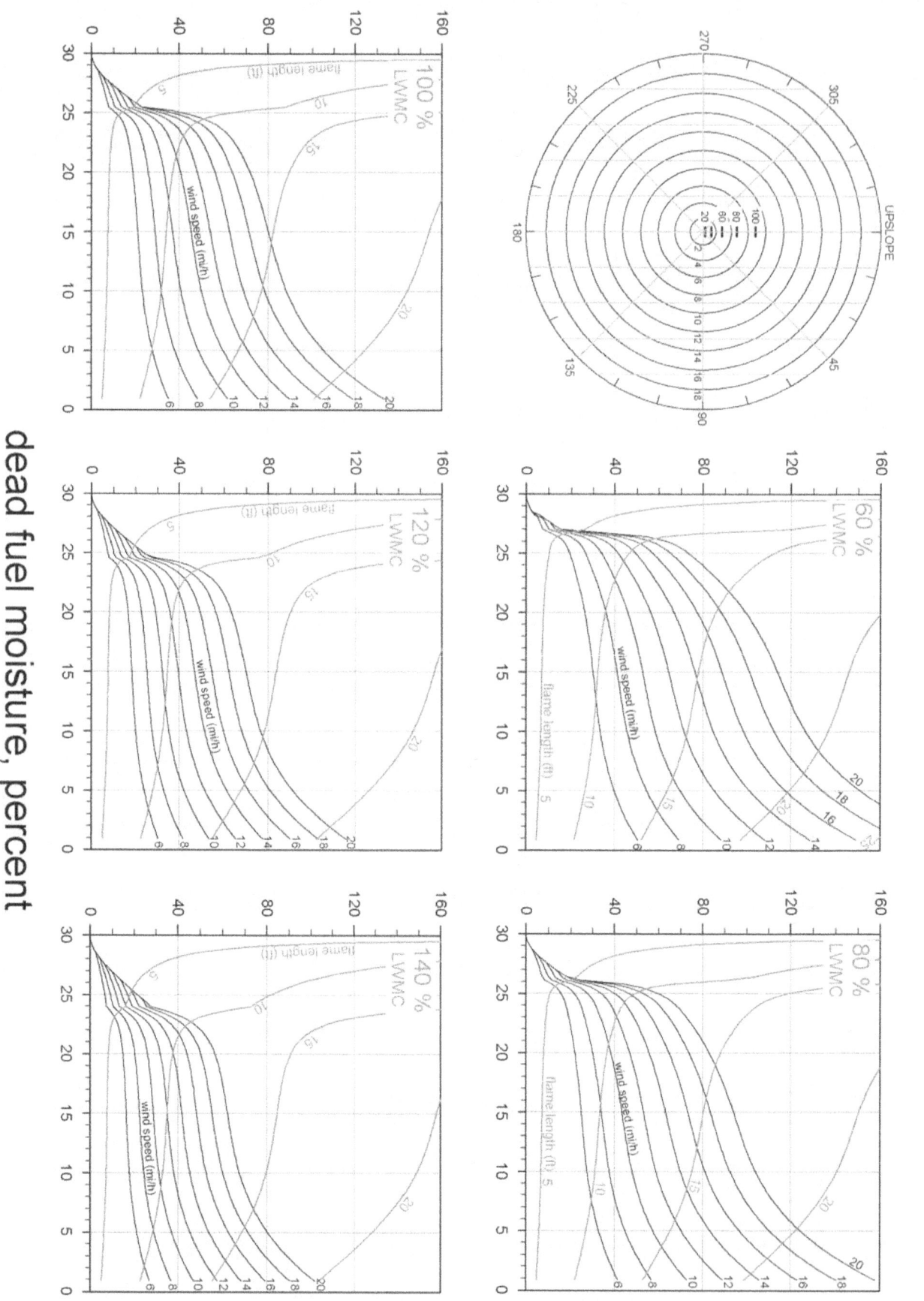

rate of spread, ch/h

dead fuel moisture, percent

SH6 (146)- high wind speeds

USDA Forest Service Gen. Tech. Rep. RMRS-GTR-192. 2007

rate of spread, ch/h

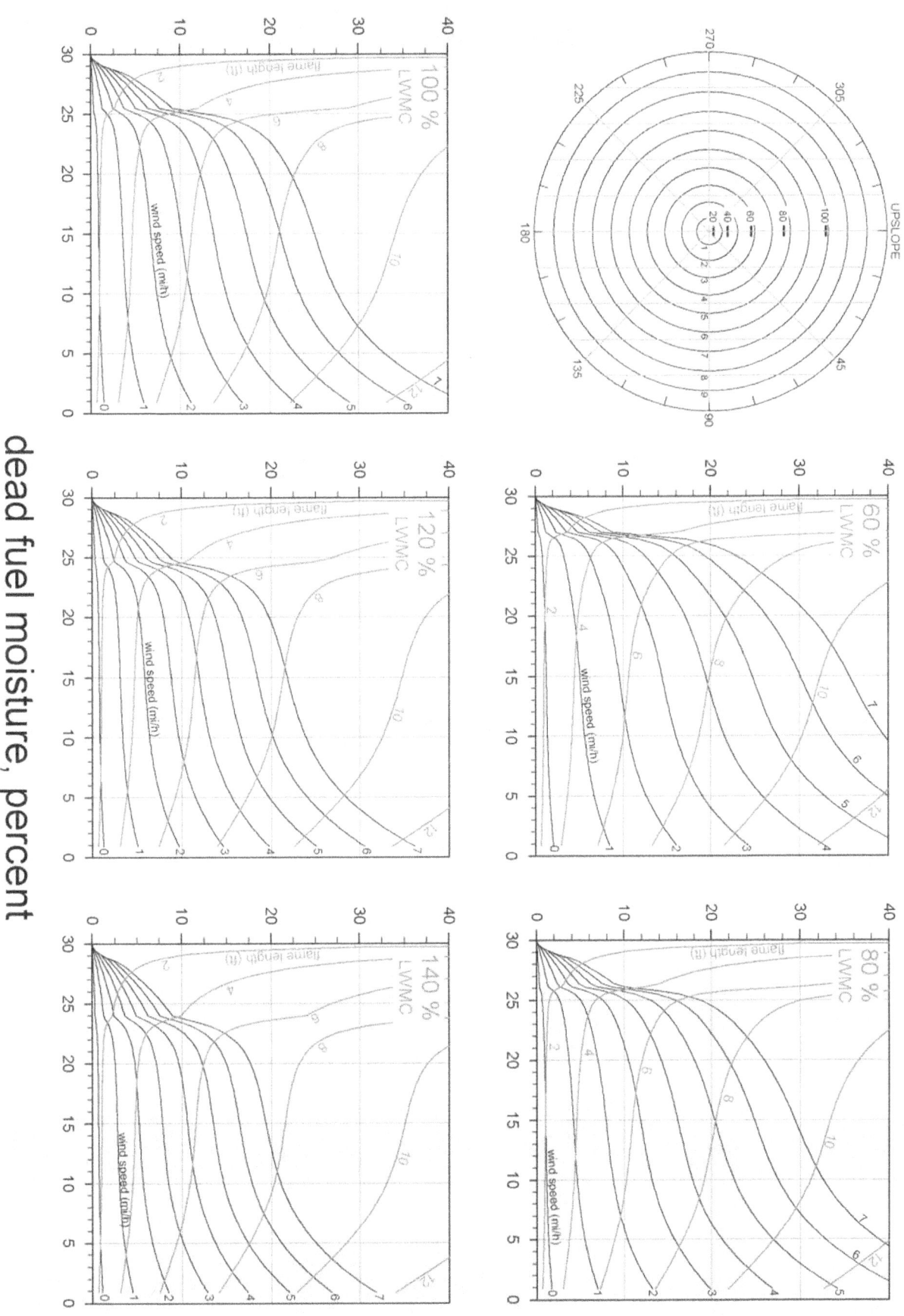

SH6 (146)- low wind speeds

dead fuel moisture, percent

USDA Forest Service Gen. Tech. Rep. RMRS-GTR-192. 2007

85

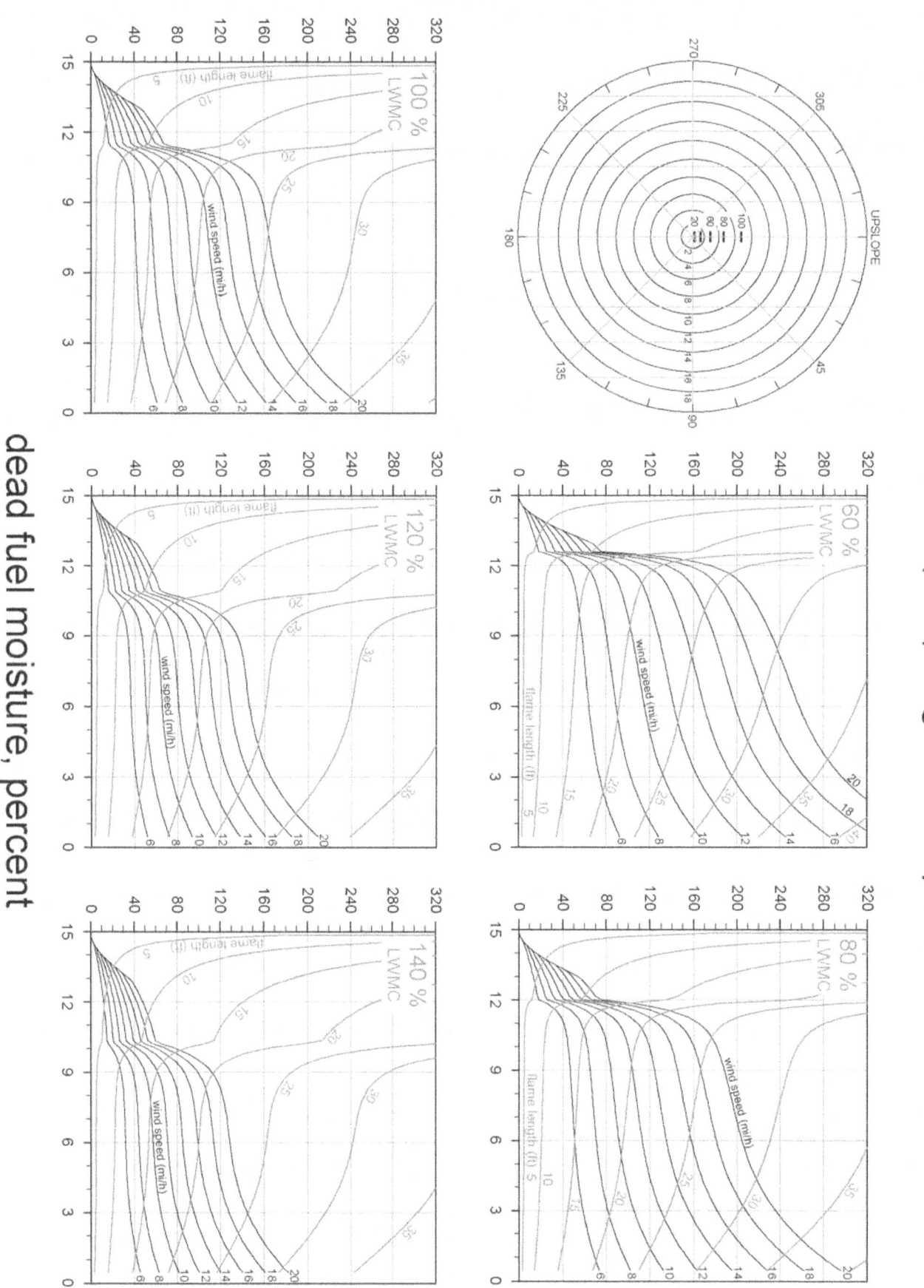

rate of spread, ch/h

dead fuel moisture, percent

SH7 (147)- high wind speeds

USDA Forest Service Gen. Tech. Rep. RMRS-GTR-192. 2007

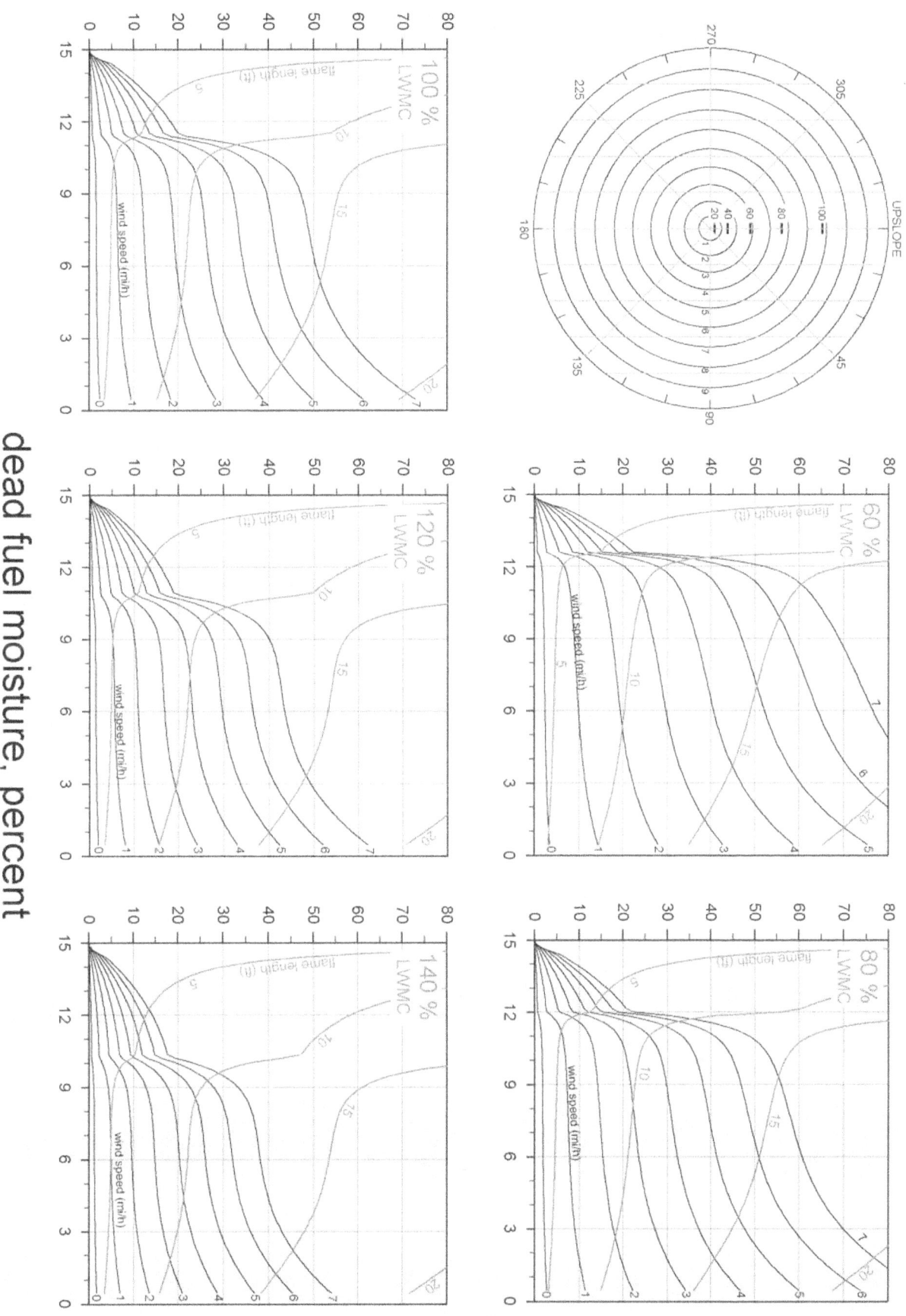

rate of spread, ch/h

dead fuel moisture, percent

SH7 (147)- low wind speeds

USDA Forest Service Gen. Tech. Rep. RMRS-GTR-192. 2007

87

rate of spread, ch/h

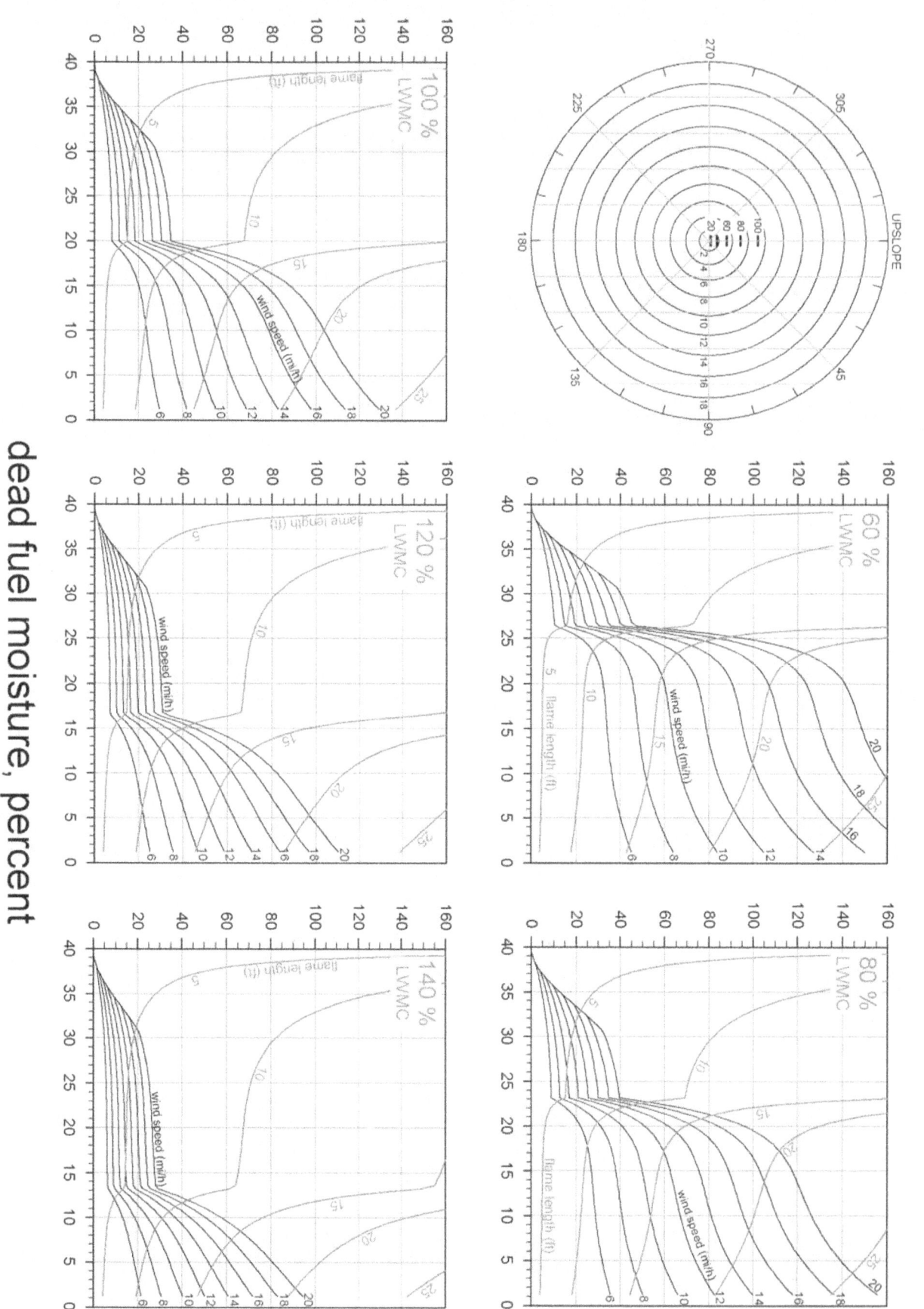

SH8 (148)- high wind speeds

dead fuel moisture, percent

88

USDA Forest Service Gen. Tech. Rep. RMRS-GTR-192. 2007

rate of spread, ch/h

SH8 (148)- low wind speeds

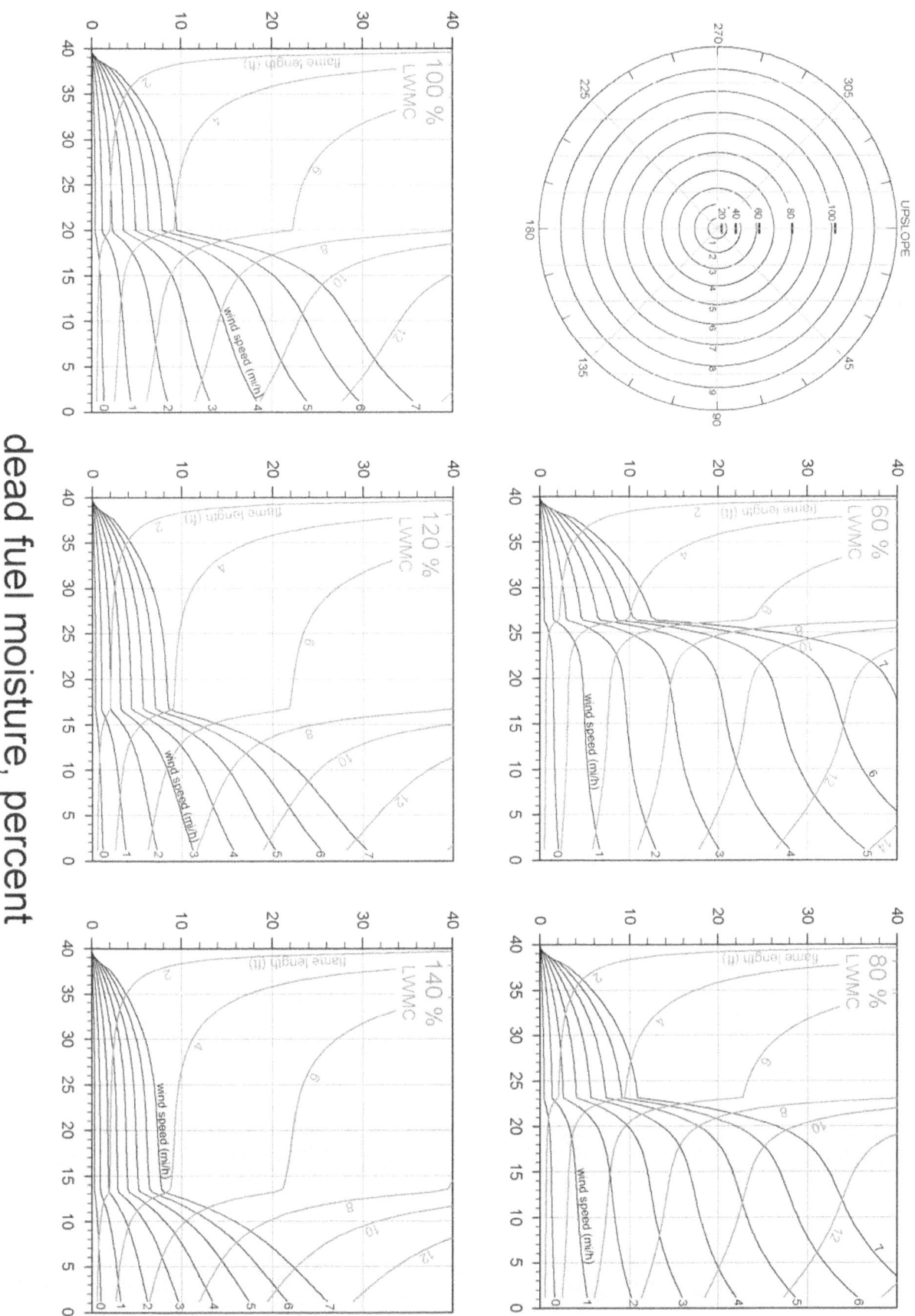

USDA Forest Service Gen. Tech. Rep. RMRS-GTR-192. 2007

89

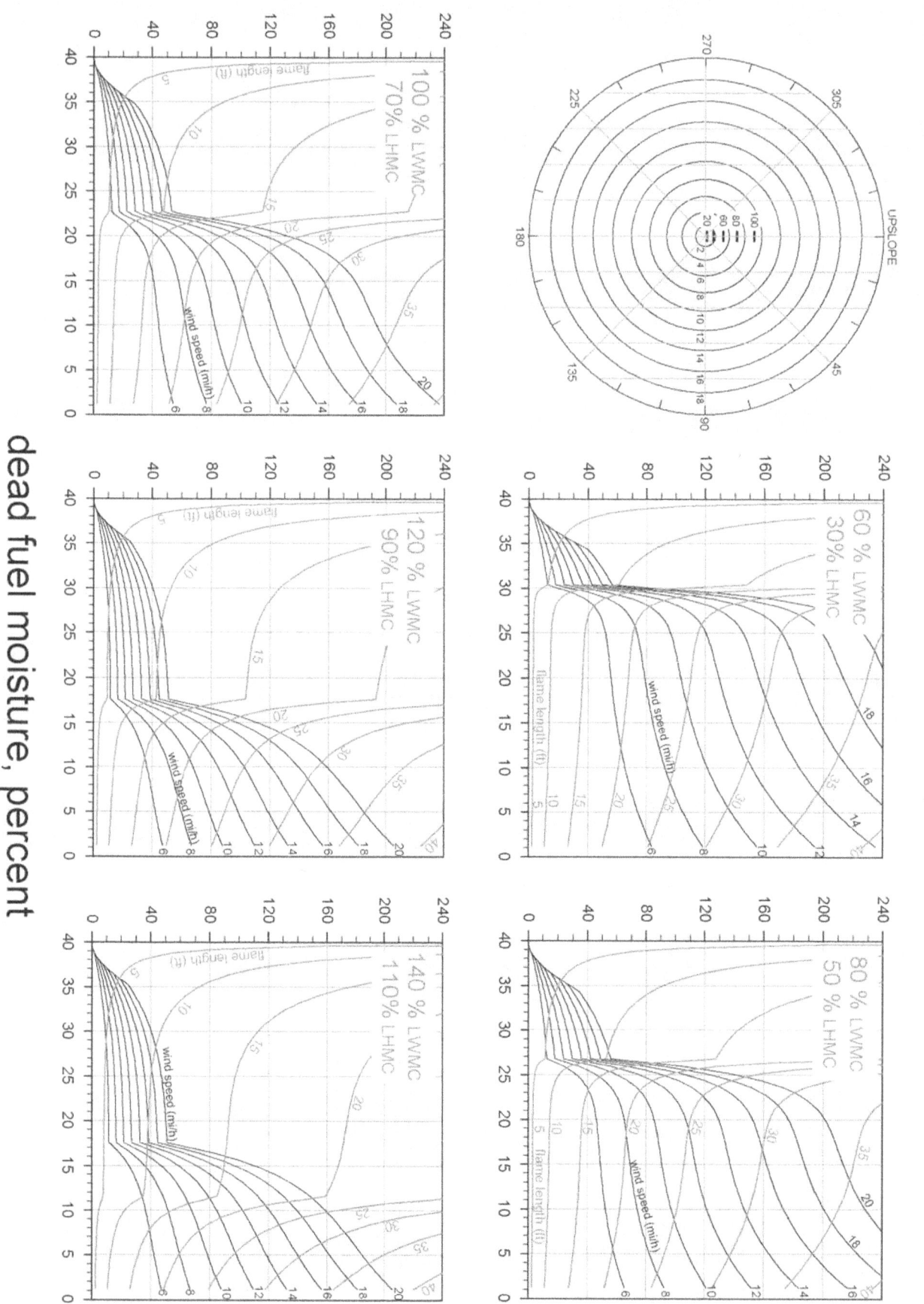

rate of spread, ch/h

dead fuel moisture, percent

SH9 (149)- high wind speeds

90

USDA Forest Service Gen. Tech. Rep. RMRS-GTR-192. 2007

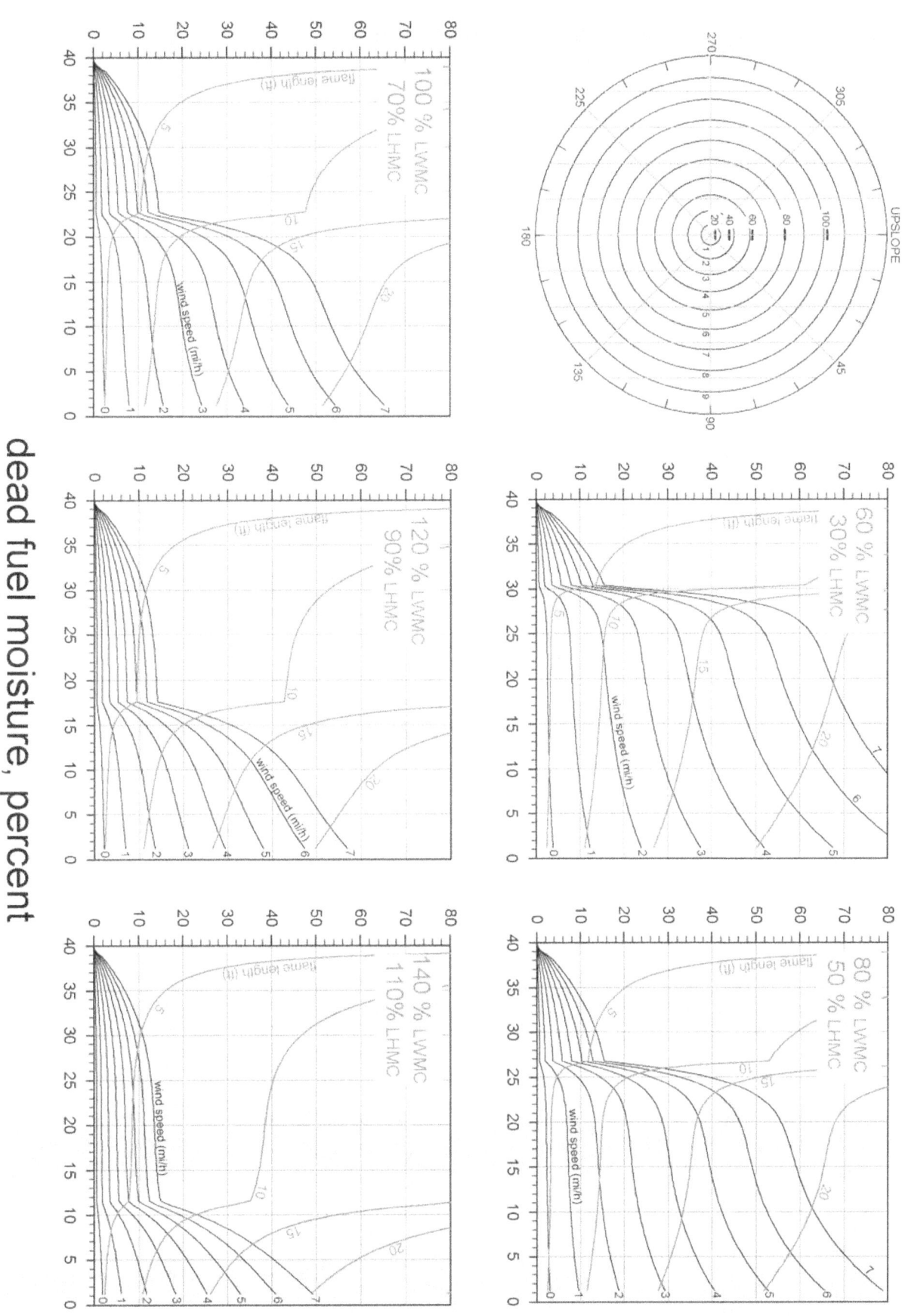

rate of spread, ch/h

dead fuel moisture, percent

SH9 (149) - low wind speeds

USDA Forest Service Gen. Tech. Rep. RMRS-GTR-192. 2007

91

Timber-understory

USDA Forest Service Gen. Tech. Rep. RMRS-GTR-192. 2007

93

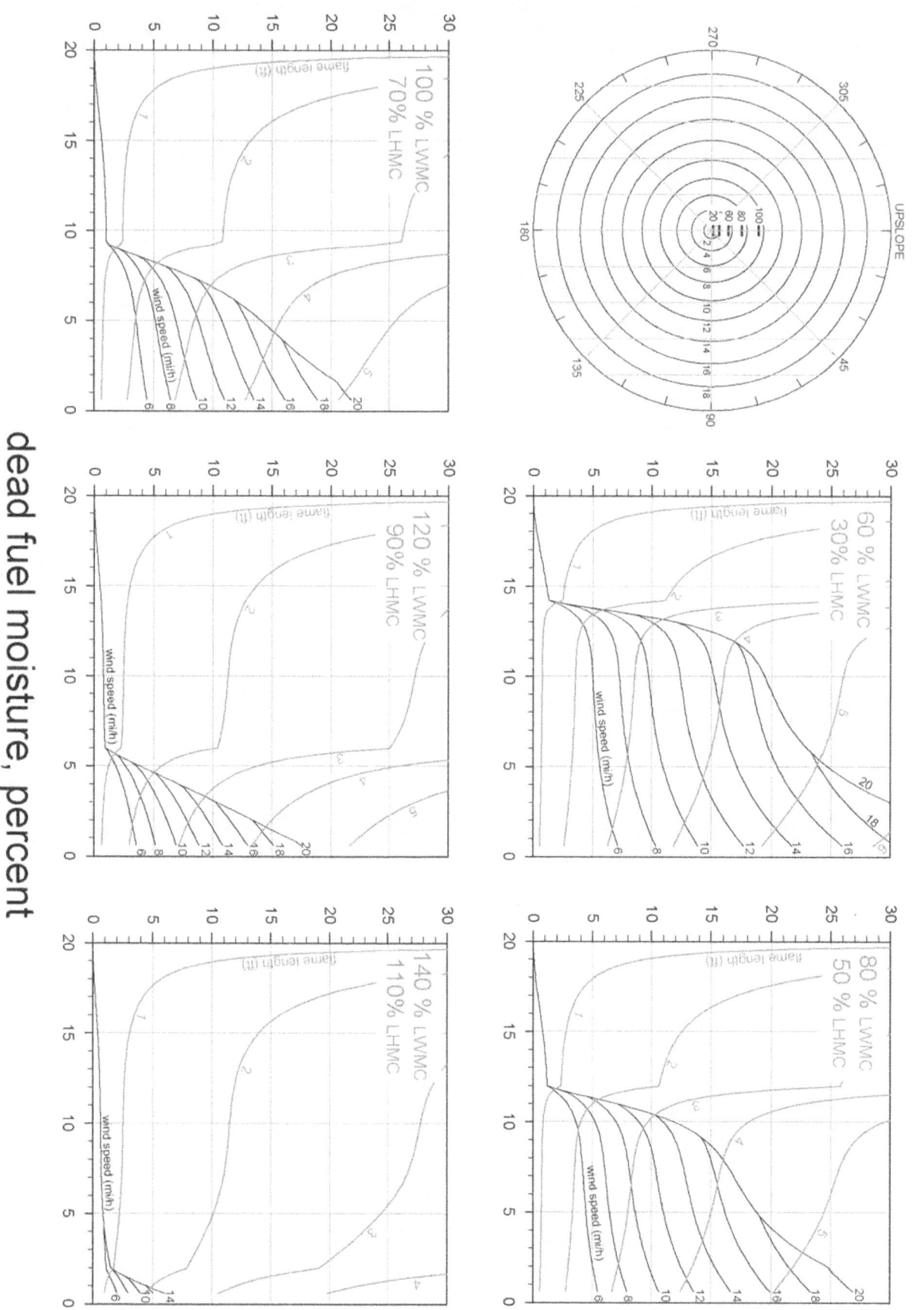

TU1 (161) - high wind speeds

rate of spread, ch/h

dead fuel moisture, percent

94

USDA Forest Service Gen. Tech. Rep. RMRS-GTR-192. 2007

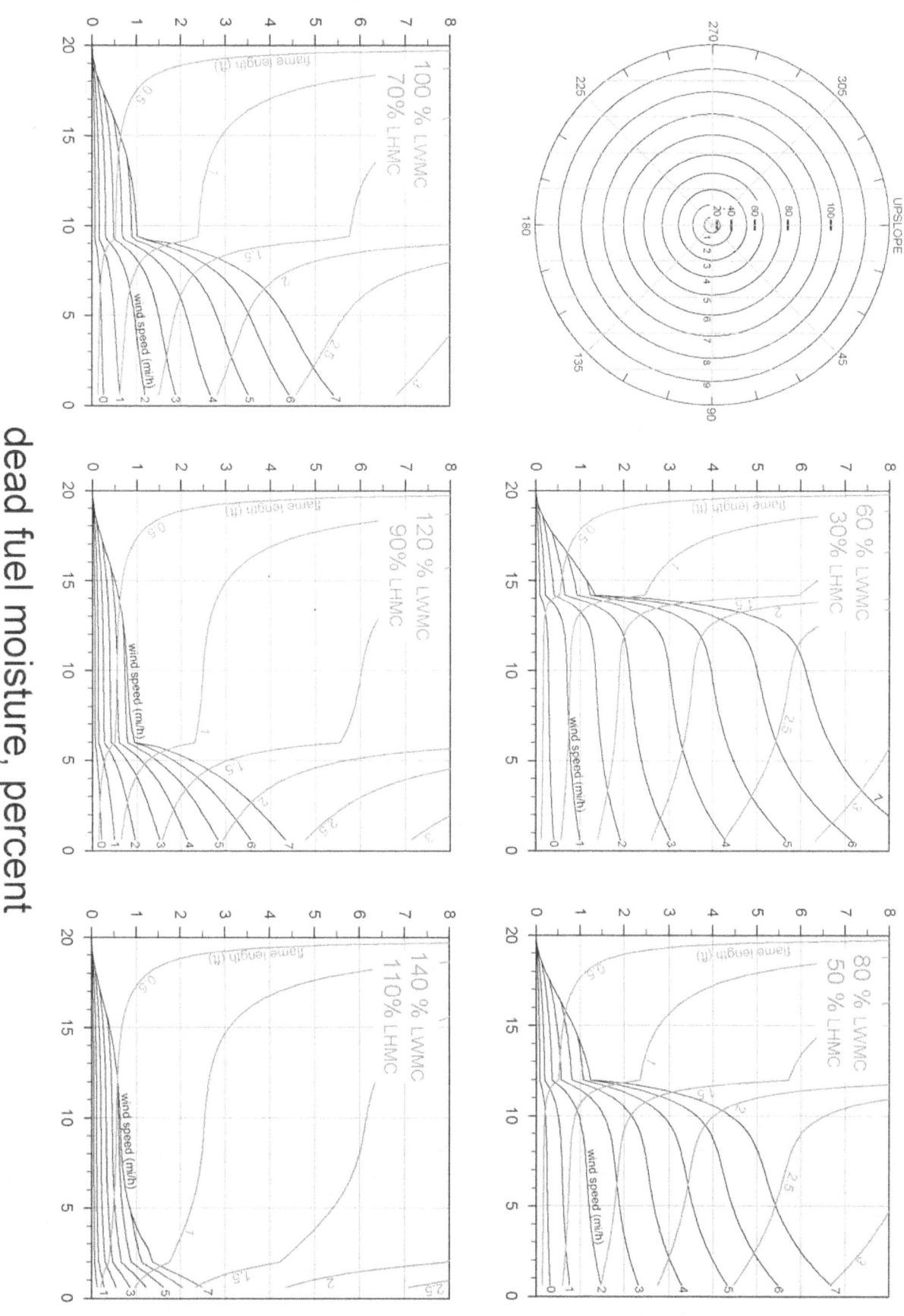

rate of spread, ch/h

dead fuel moisture, percent

TU1 (161) - low wind speeds

USDA Forest Service Gen. Tech. Rep. RMRS-GTR-192. 2007

95

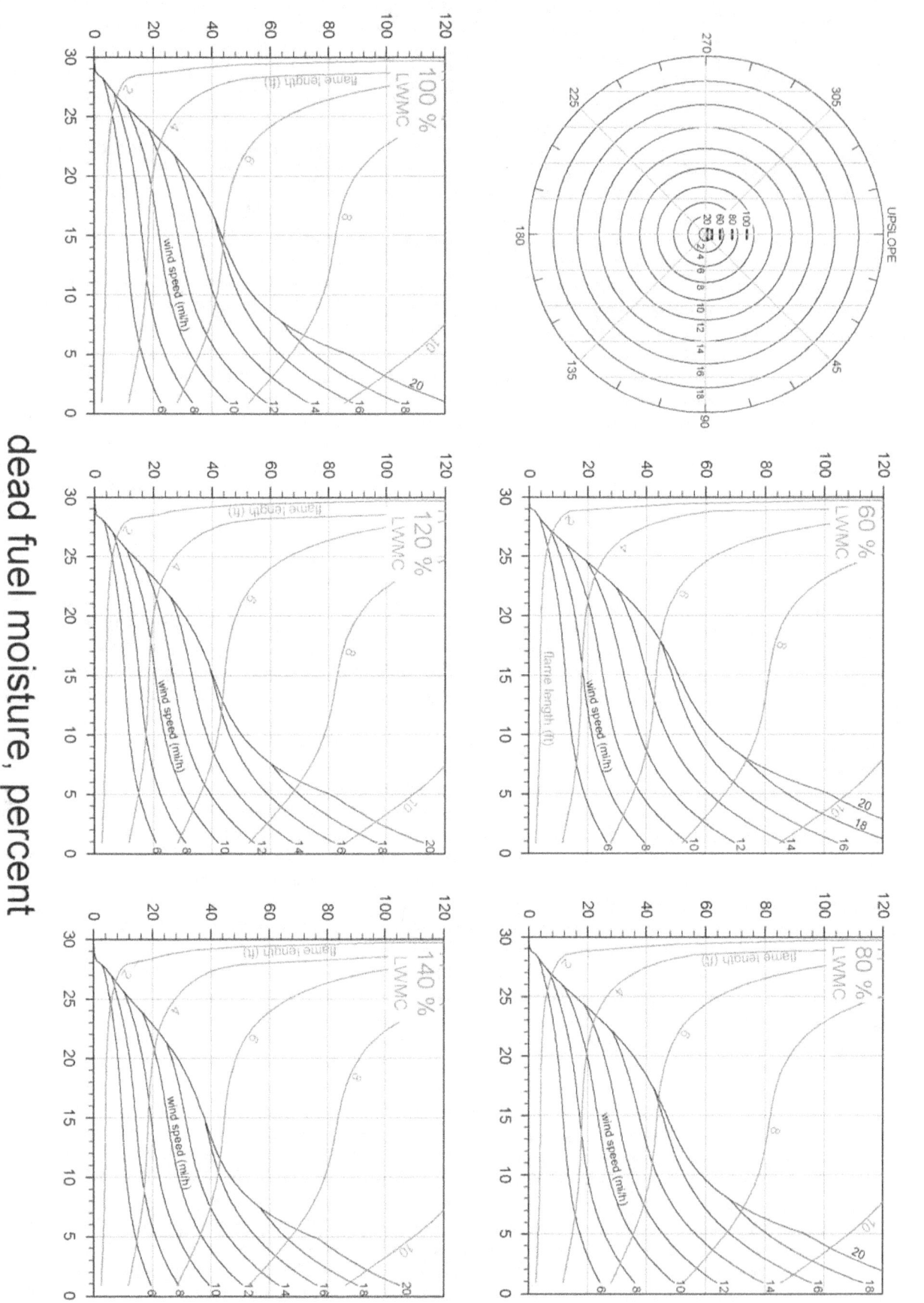

rate of spread, ch/h

dead fuel moisture, percent

TU2 (162) - high wind speeds

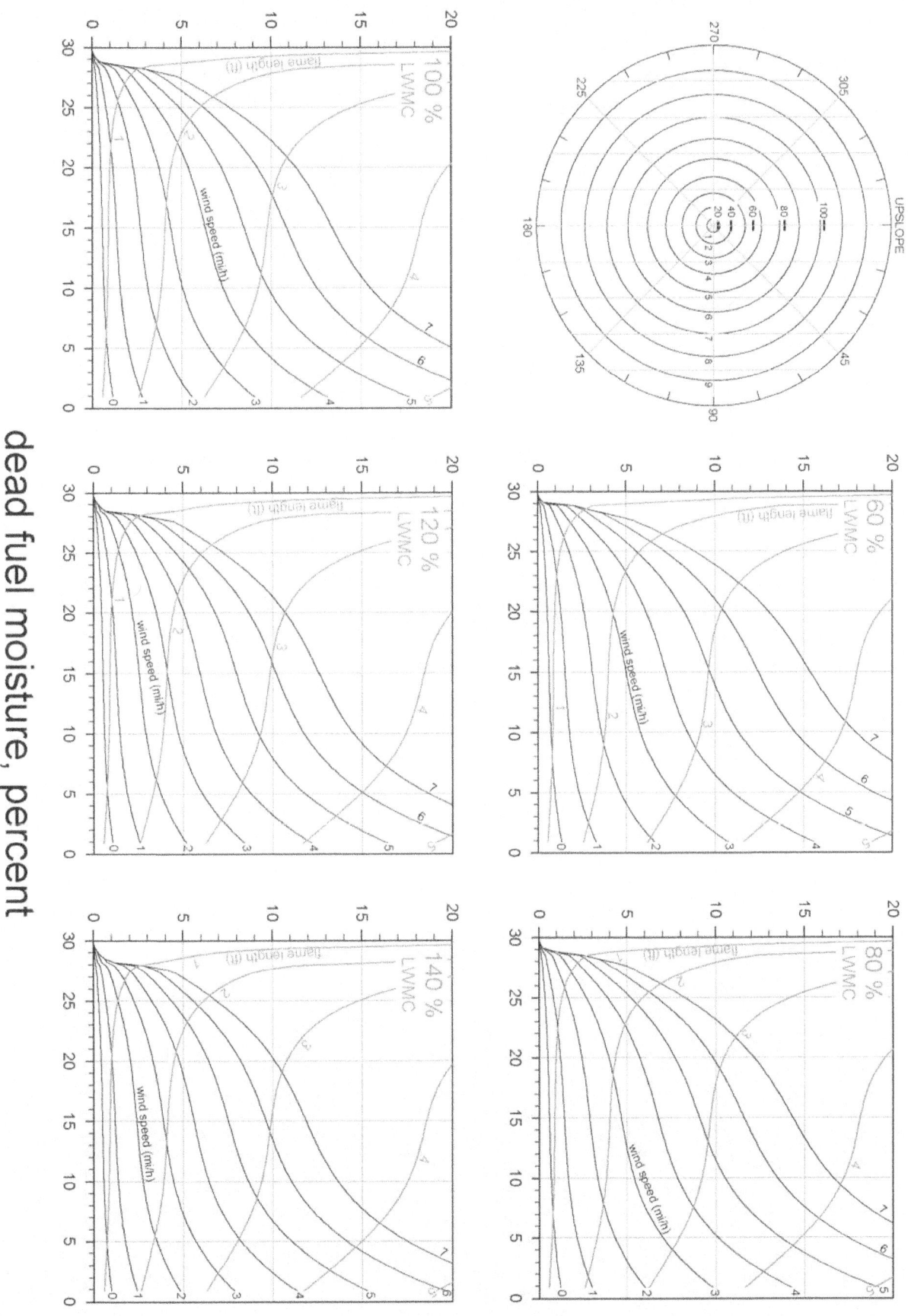

rate of spread, ch/h

dead fuel moisture, percent

TU2 (162) - low wind speeds

USDA Forest Service Gen. Tech. Rep. RMRS-GTR-192. 2007

97

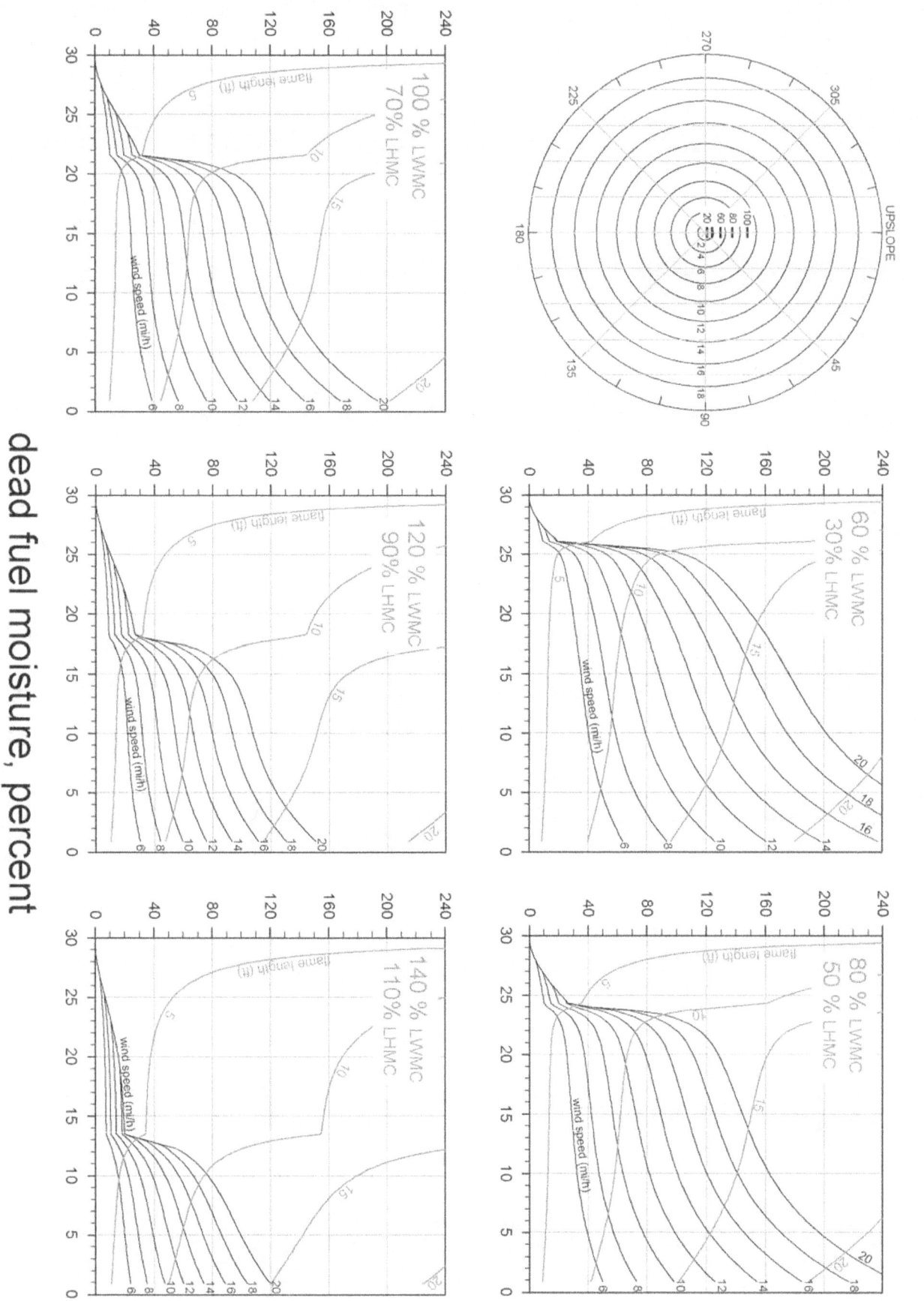

rate of spread, ch/h

TU3 (163) - high wind speeds

dead fuel moisture, percent

98

USDA Forest Service Gen. Tech. Rep. RMRS-GTR-192. 2007

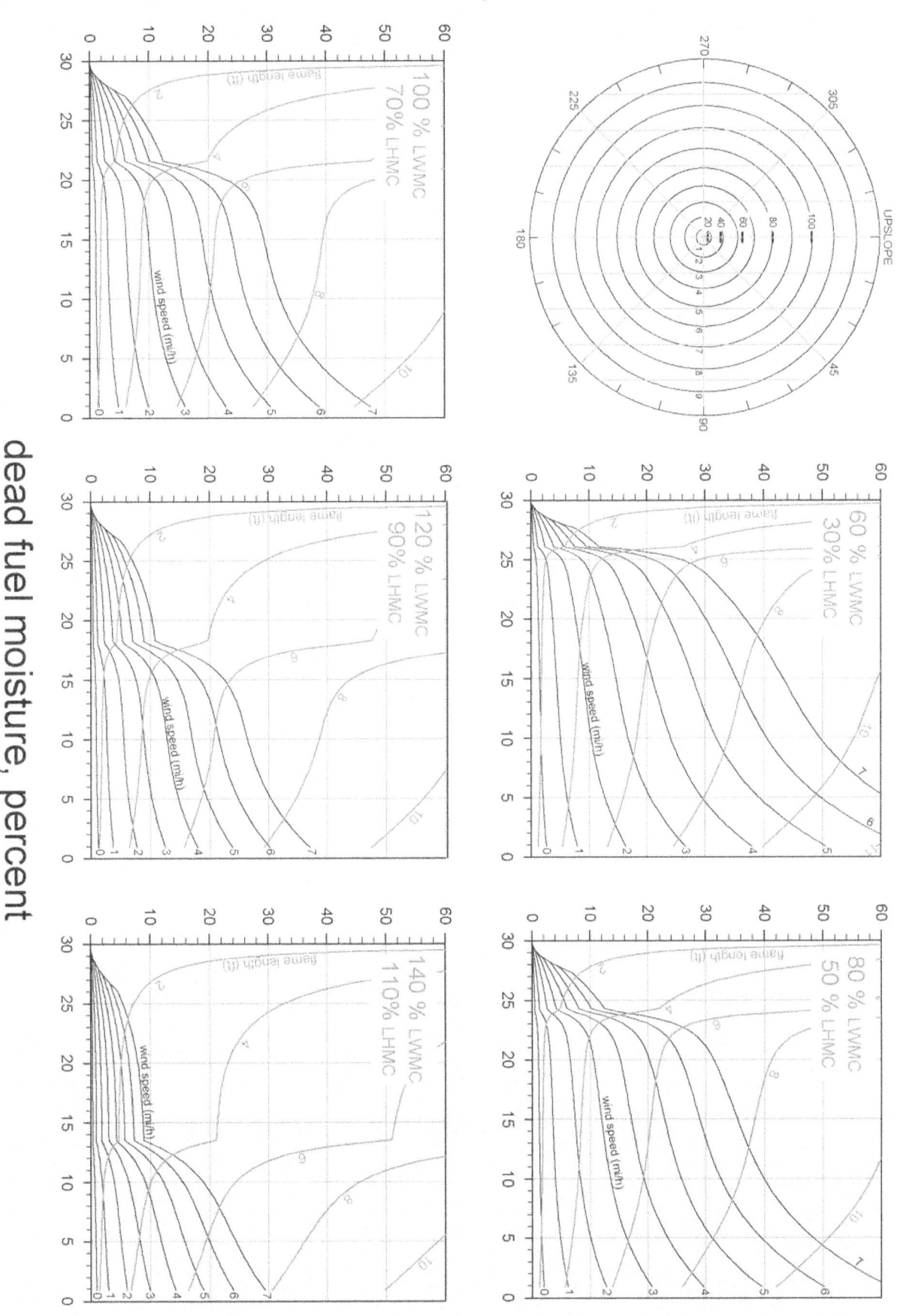

TU3 (163) - low wind speeds

rate of spread, ch/h

dead fuel moisture, percent

USDA Forest Service Gen. Tech. Rep. RMRS-GTR-192. 2007

99

rate of spread, ch/h

dead fuel moisture, percent

TU4 (164) - high wind speeds

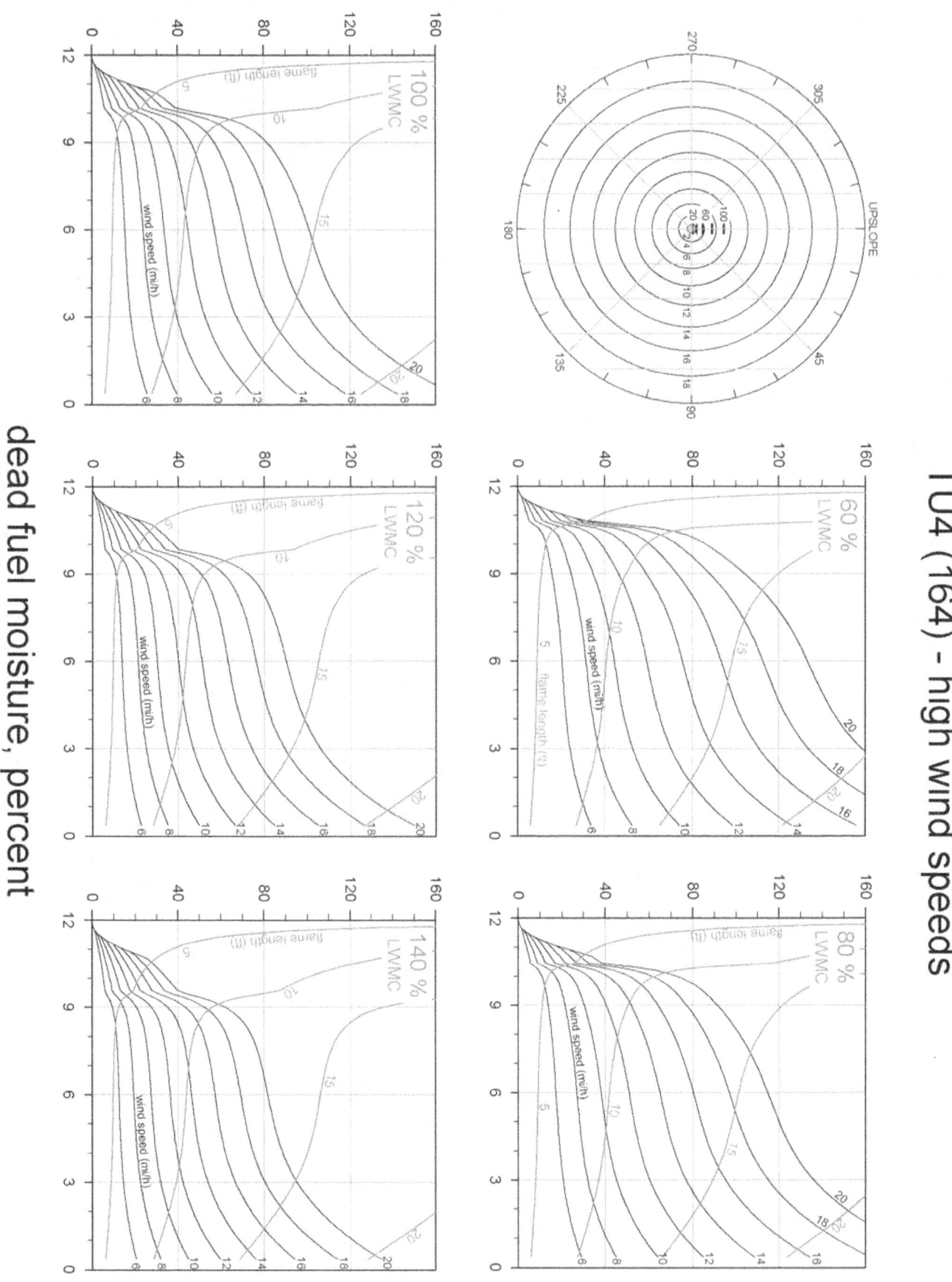

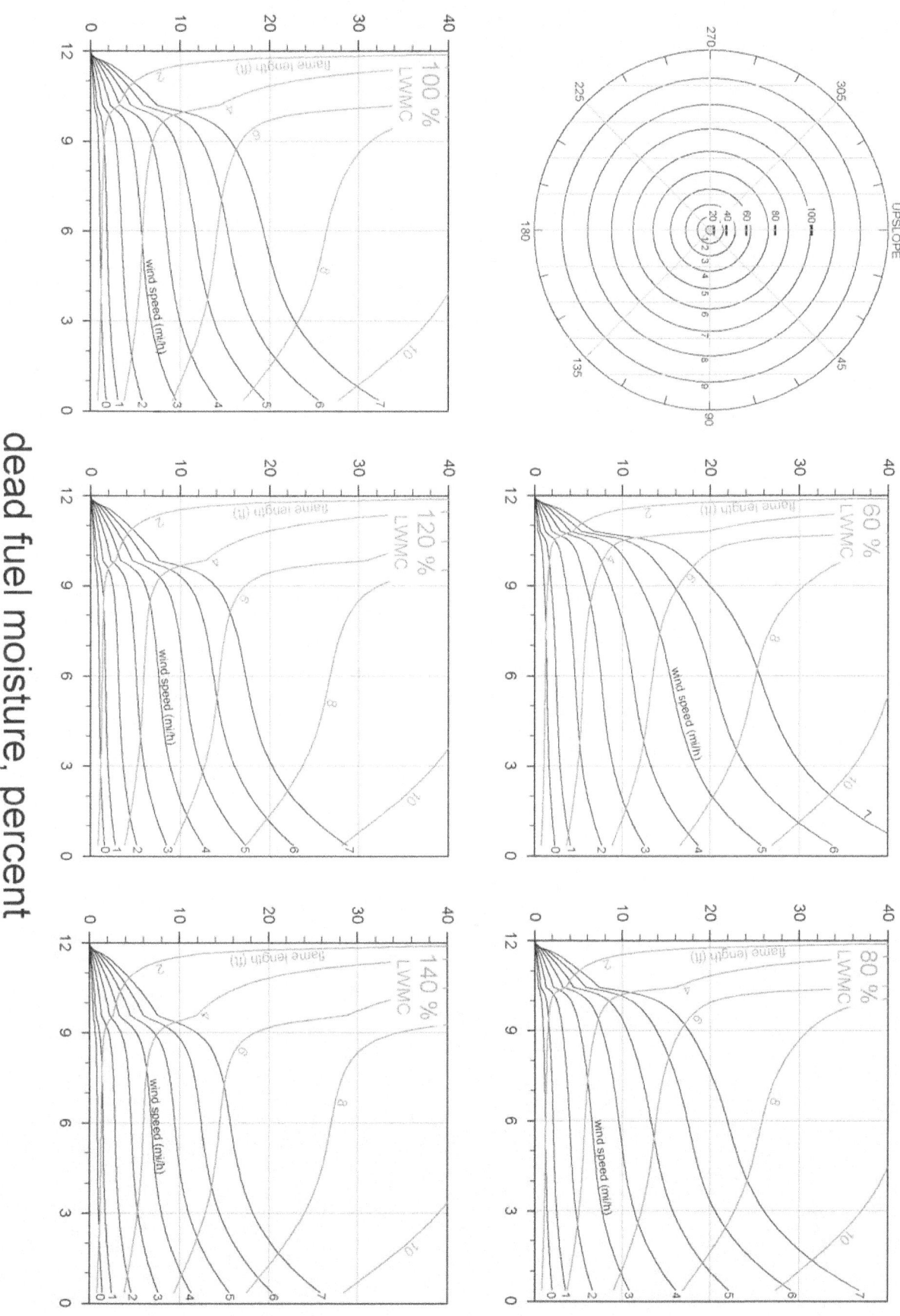

rate of spread, ch/h

dead fuel moisture, percent

TU4 (164) - low wind speeds

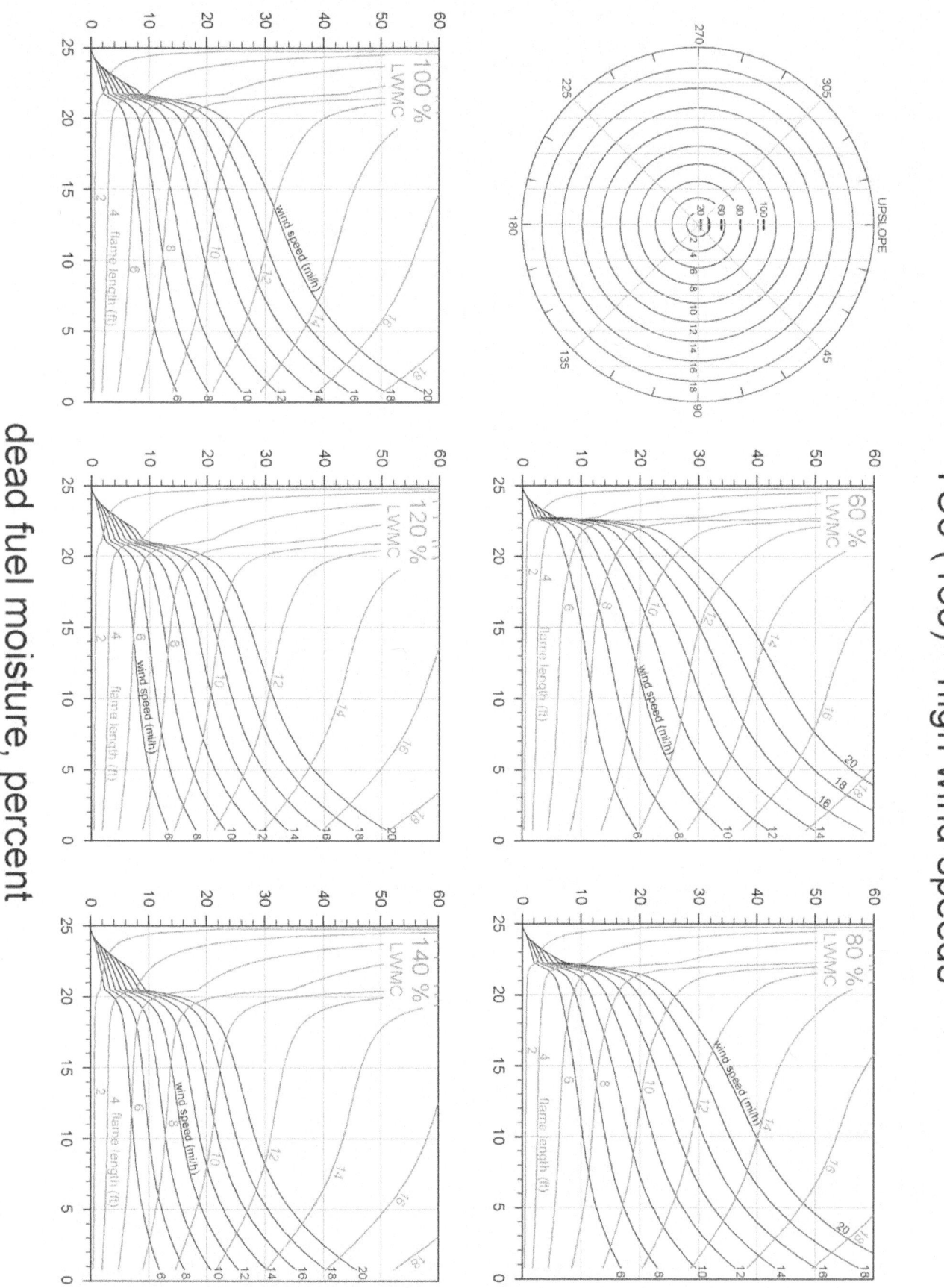

rate of spread, ch/h

dead fuel moisture, percent

TU5 (165) - high wind speeds

USDA Forest Service Gen. Tech. Rep. RMRS-GTR-192. 2007

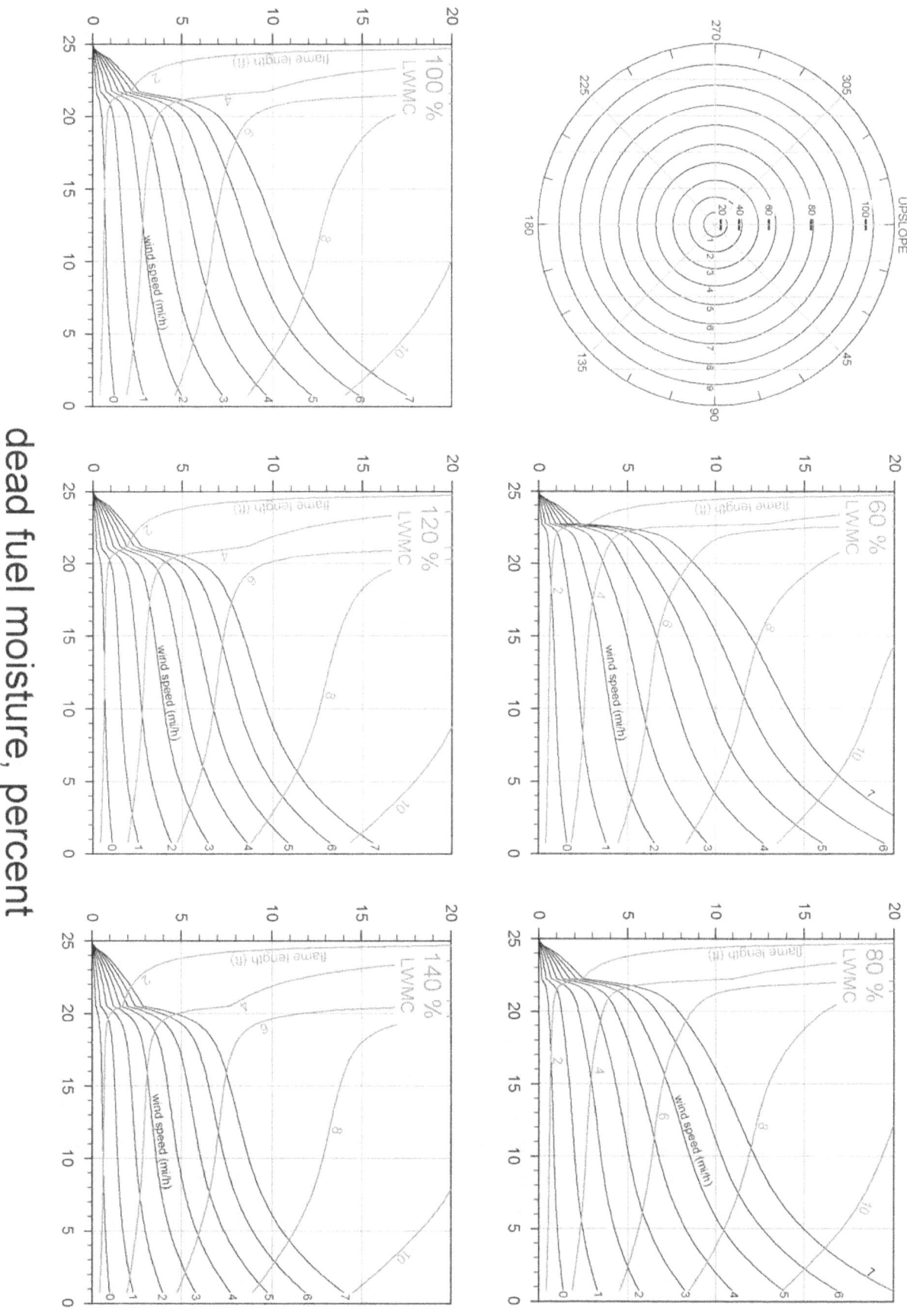

rate of spread, ch/h

dead fuel moisture, percent

TU5 (165) - low wind speeds

USDA Forest Service Gen. Tech. Rep. RMRS-GTR-192. 2007

103

Timber litter

USDA Forest Service Gen. Tech. Rep. RMRS-GTR-192. 2007

105

TL1 (181)

low wind speeds

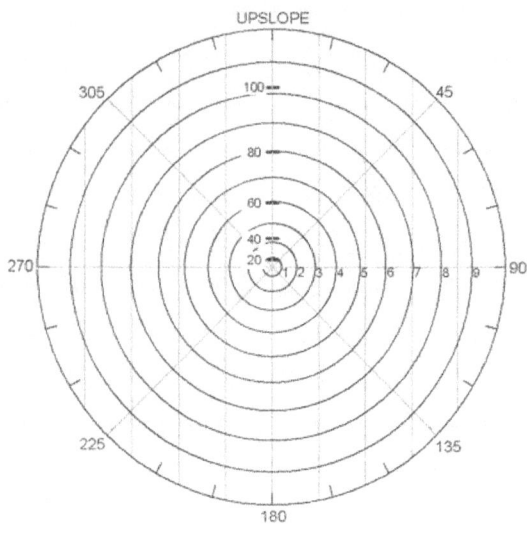

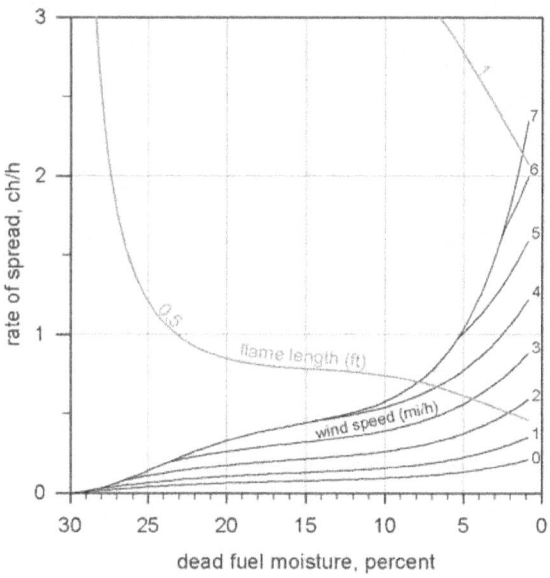

high wind speeds

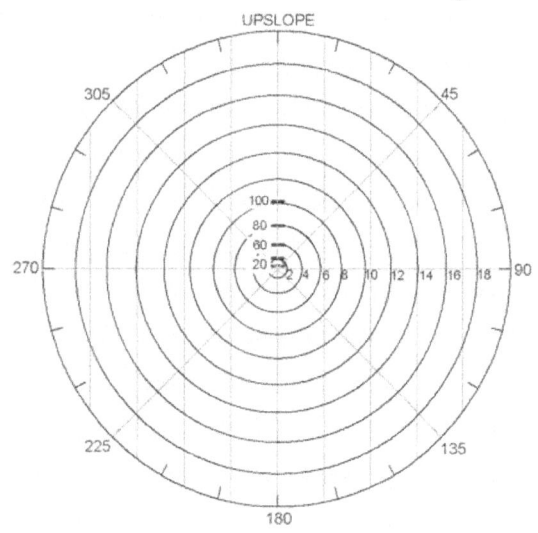

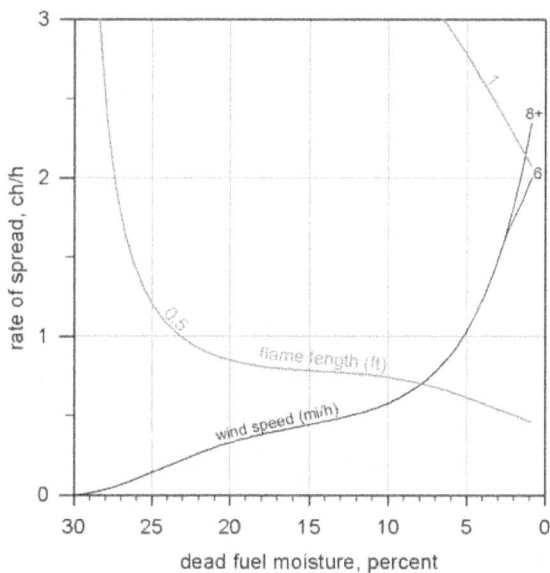

USDA Forest Service Gen. Tech. Rep. RMRS-GTR-192. 2007

TL2 (182)

low wind speeds

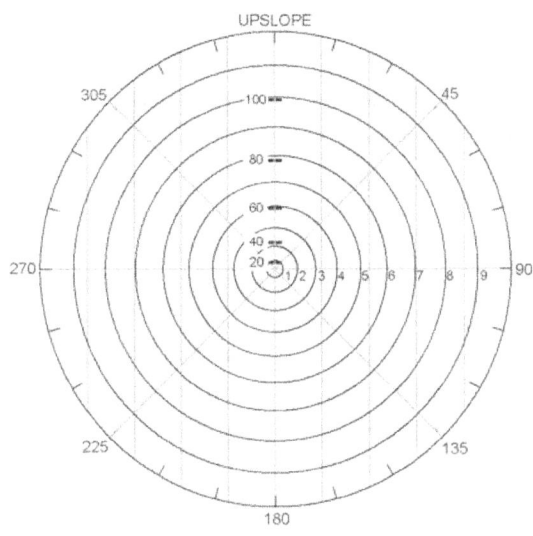

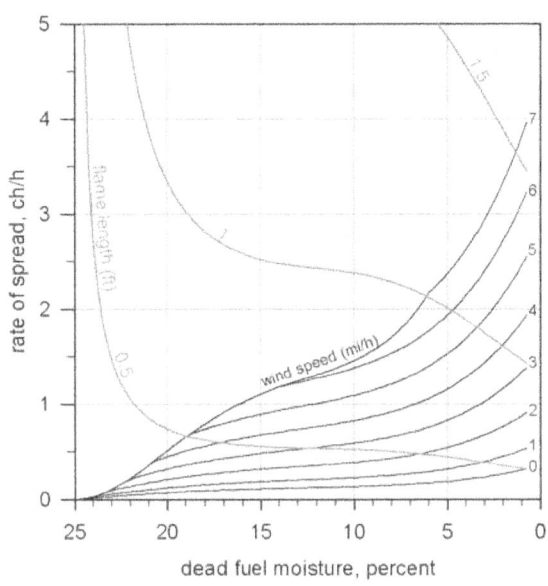

high wind speeds

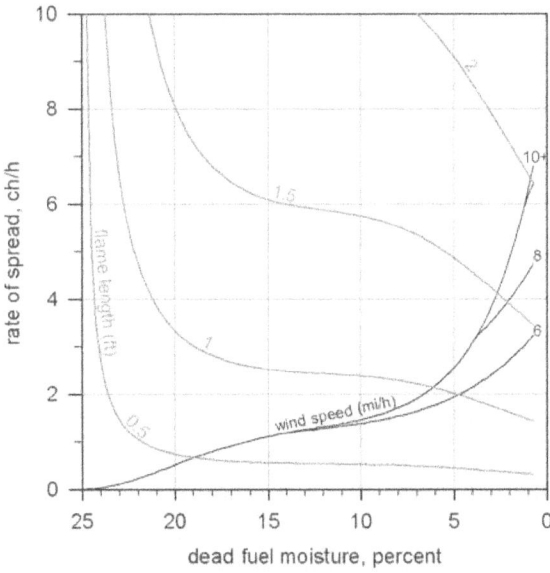

USDA Forest Service Gen. Tech. Rep. RMRS-GTR-192. 2007

107

TL3 (183)

low wind speeds

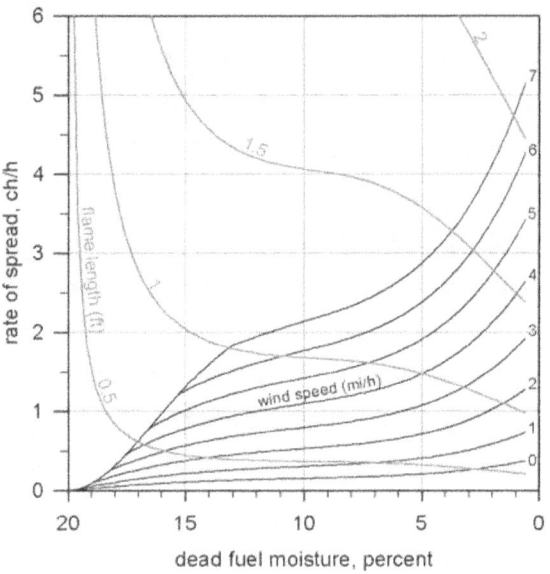

high wind speeds

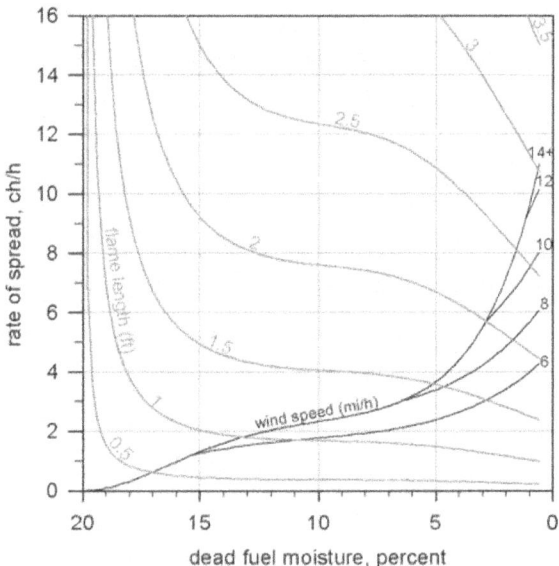

USDA Forest Service Gen. Tech. Rep. RMRS-GTR-192. 2007

TL4 (184)

low wind speeds

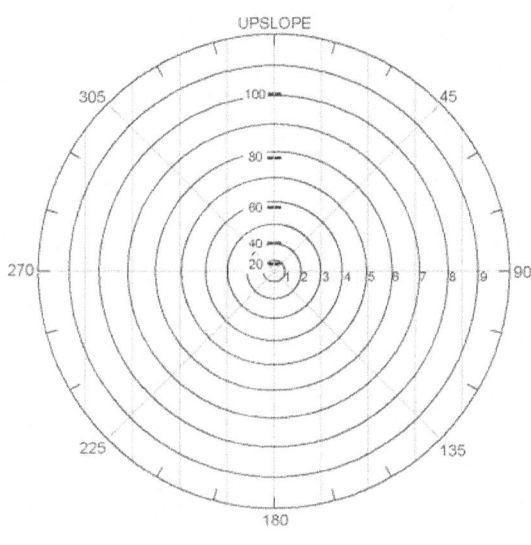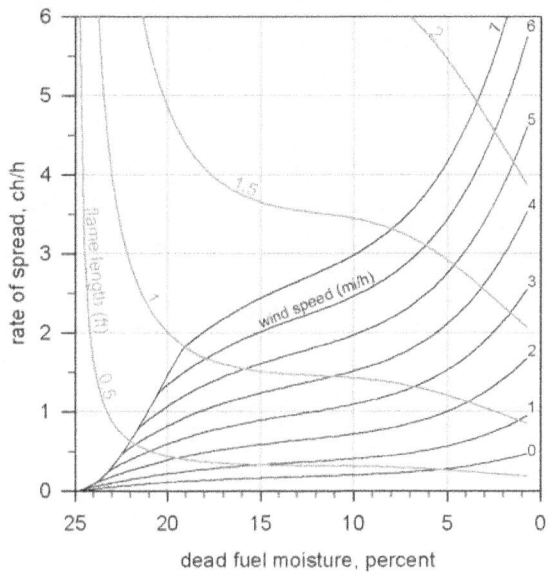

high wind speeds

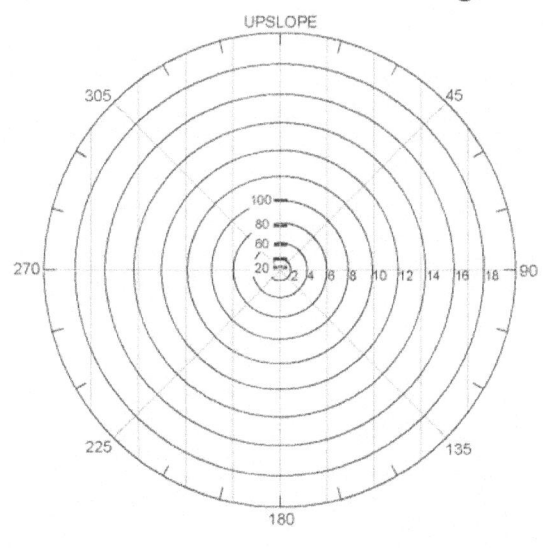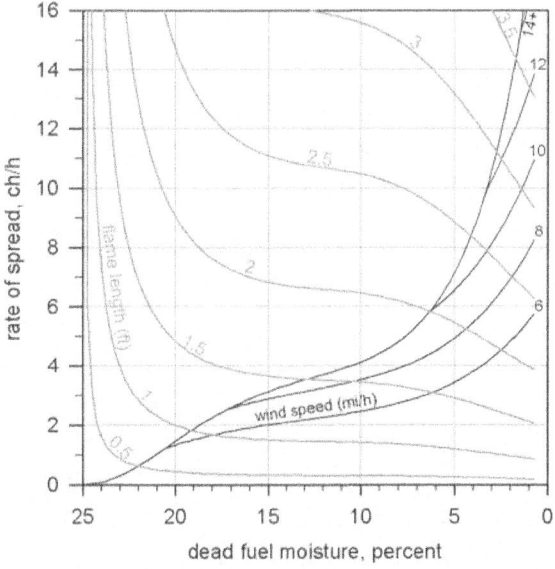

USDA Forest Service Gen. Tech. Rep. RMRS-GTR-192. 2007

109

TL5 (185)

low wind speeds

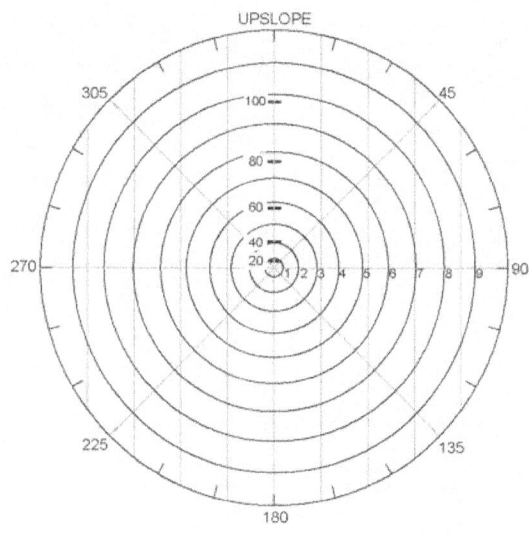
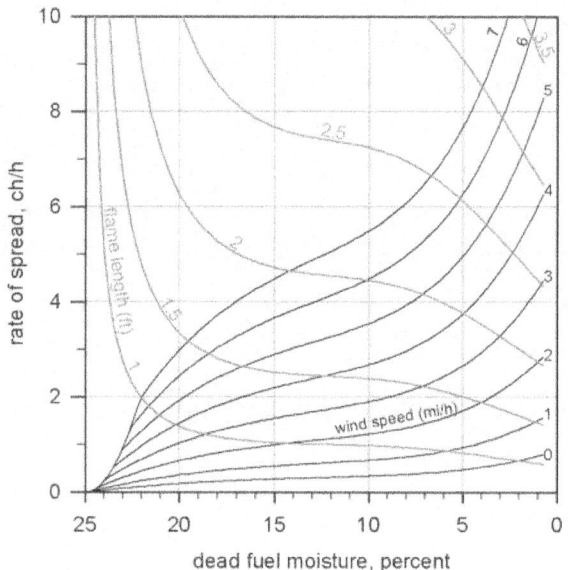

high wind speeds

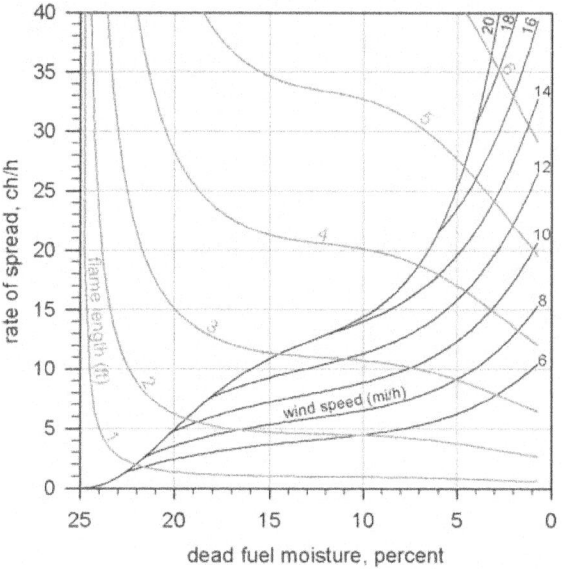

USDA Forest Service Gen. Tech. Rep. RMRS-GTR-192. 2007

TL6 (186)

low wind speeds

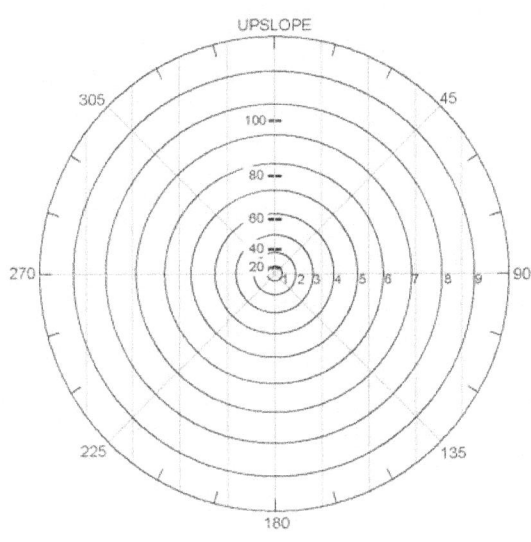

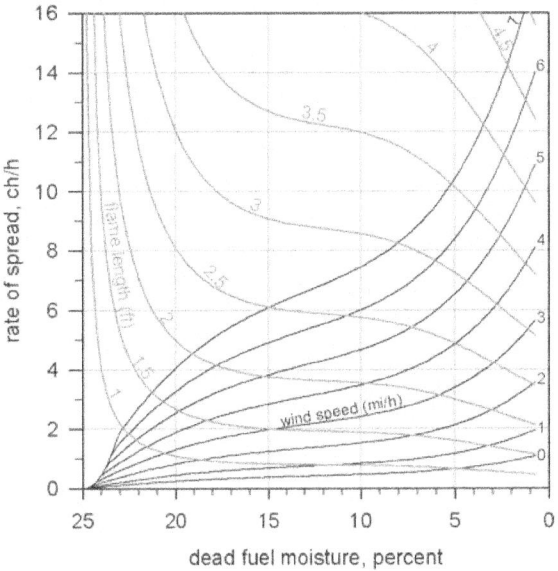

high wind speeds

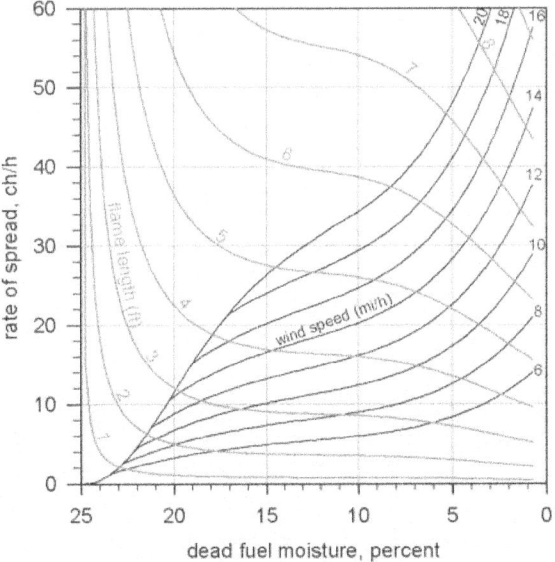

USDA Forest Service Gen. Tech. Rep. RMRS-GTR-192. 2007

111

TL7 (187)

low wind speeds

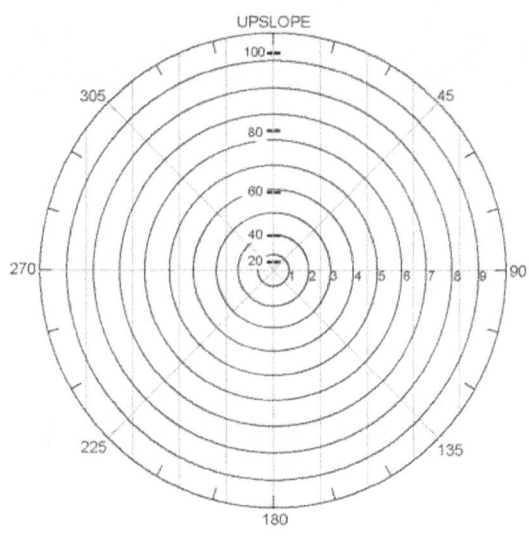

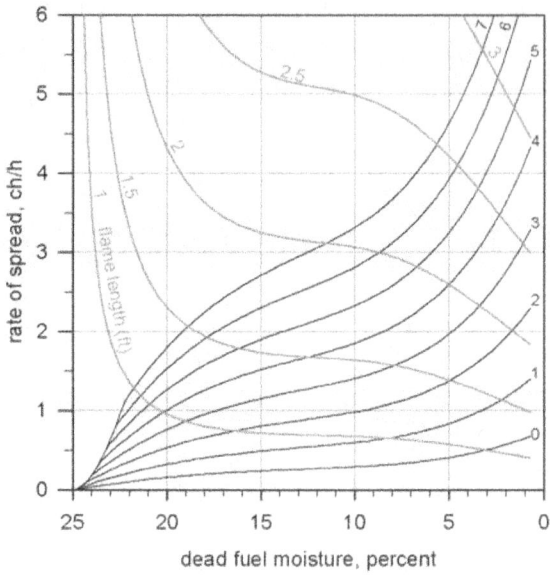

high wind speeds

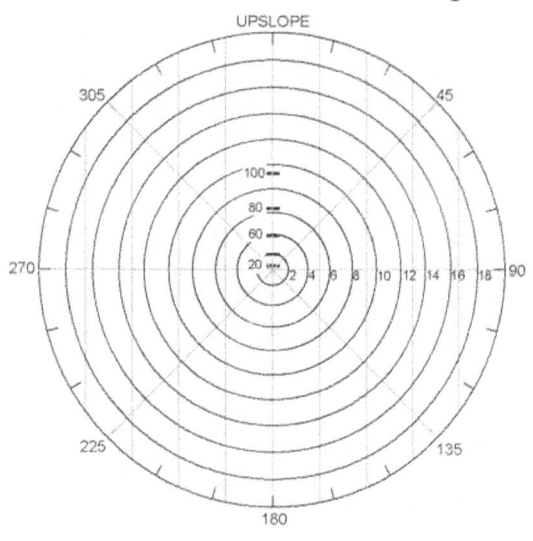

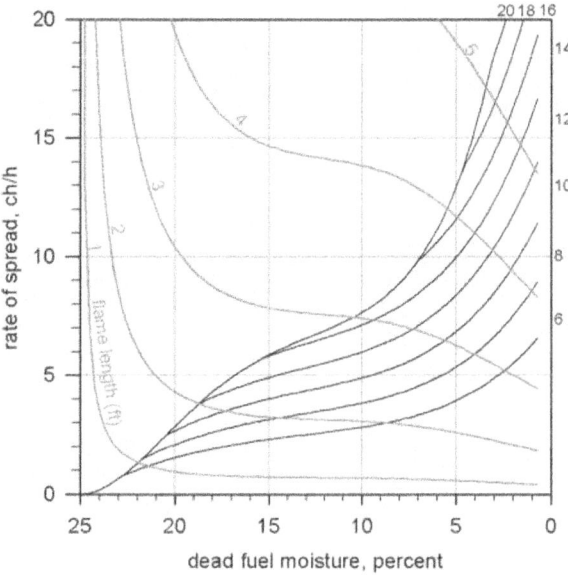

USDA Forest Service Gen. Tech. Rep. RMRS-GTR-192. 2007

TL8 (188)

low wind speeds

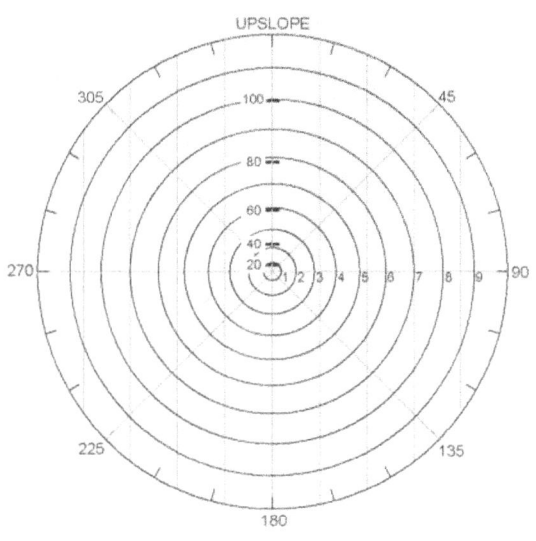

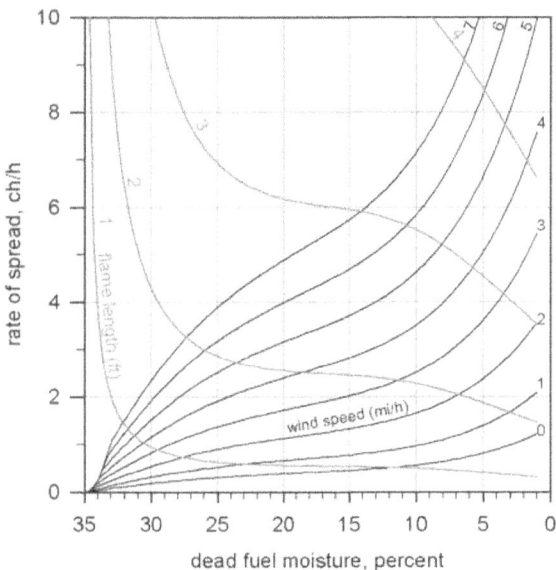

high wind speeds

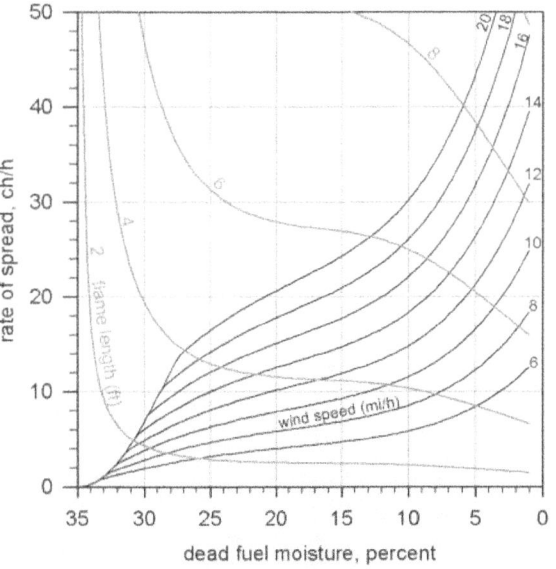

USDA Forest Service Gen. Tech. Rep. RMRS-GTR-192. 2007

113

TL9 (189)

low wind speeds

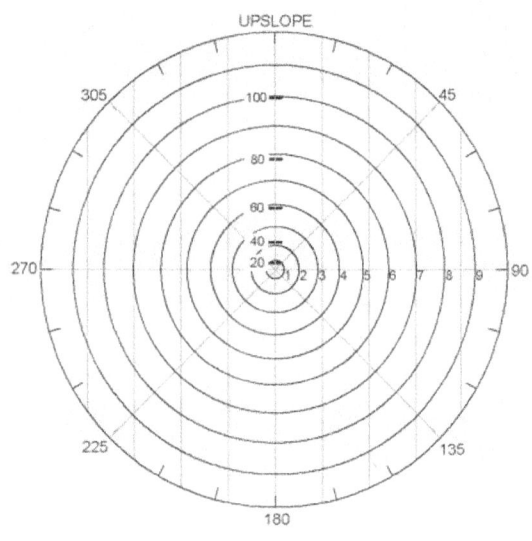

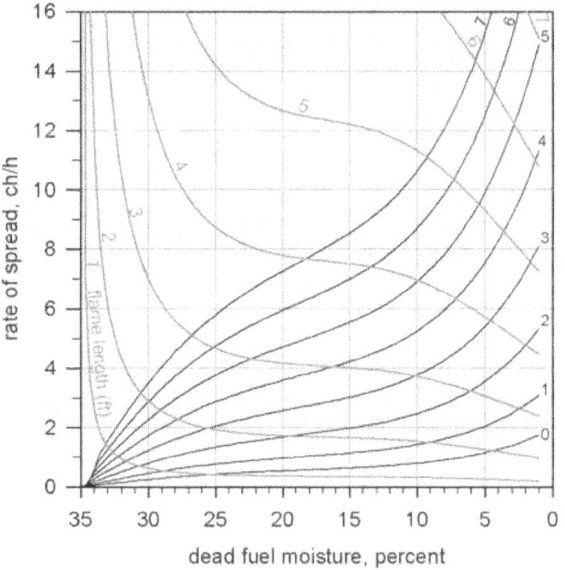

high wind speeds

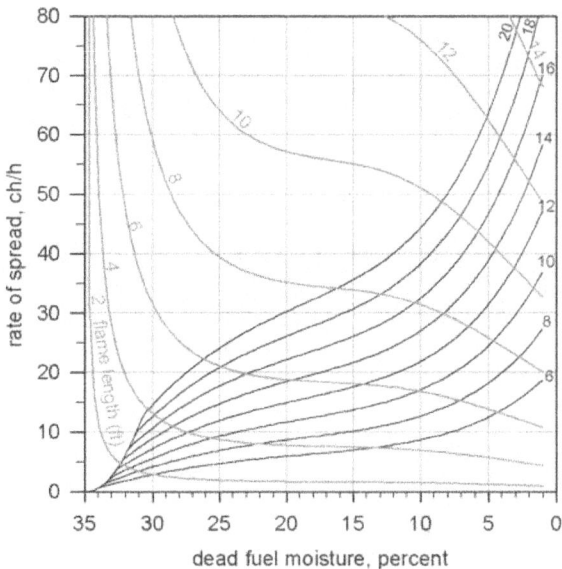

USDA Forest Service Gen. Tech. Rep. RMRS-GTR-192. 2007

Slash-blowdown

USDA Forest Service Gen. Tech. Rep. RMRS-GTR-192. 2007

115

SB1 (201)

low wind speeds

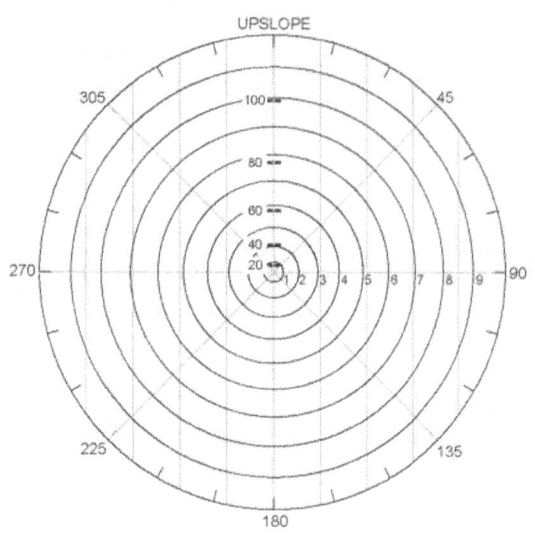

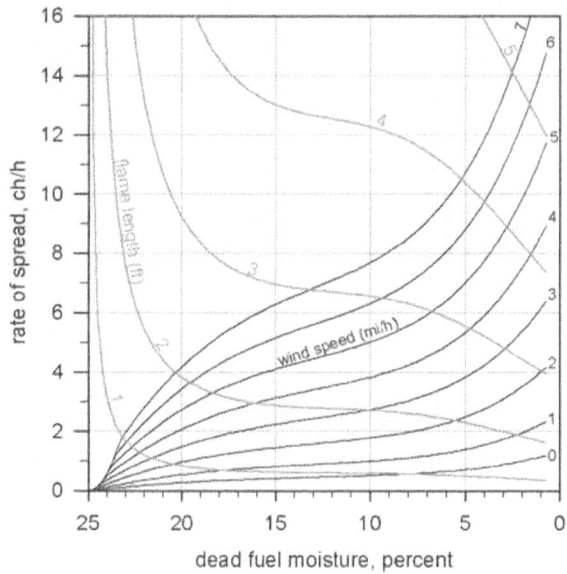

high wind speeds

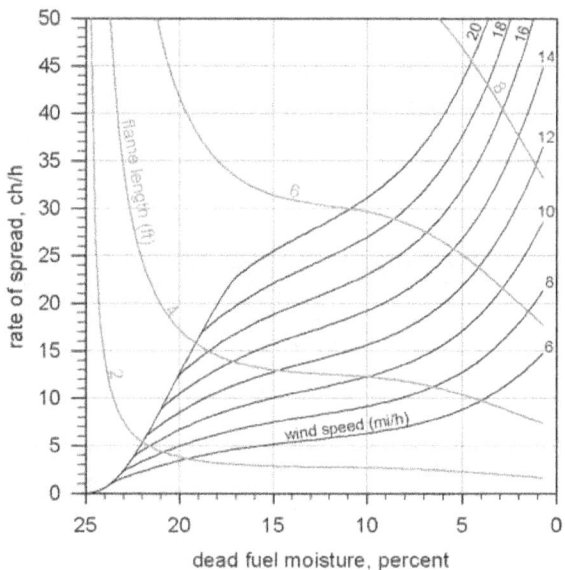

USDA Forest Service Gen. Tech. Rep. RMRS-GTR-192. 2007

SB2 (202)

low wind speeds

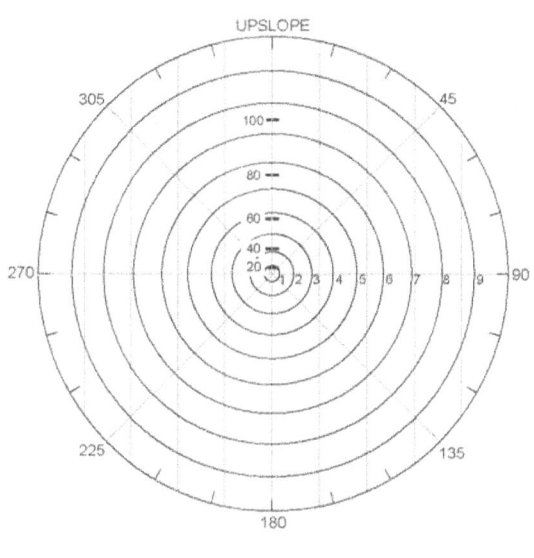

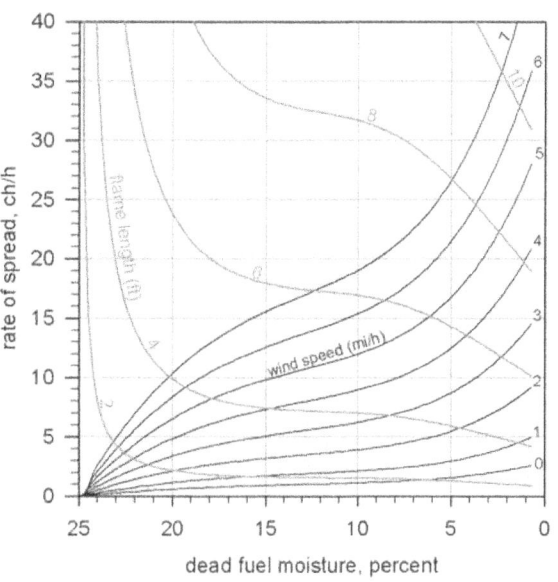

high wind speeds

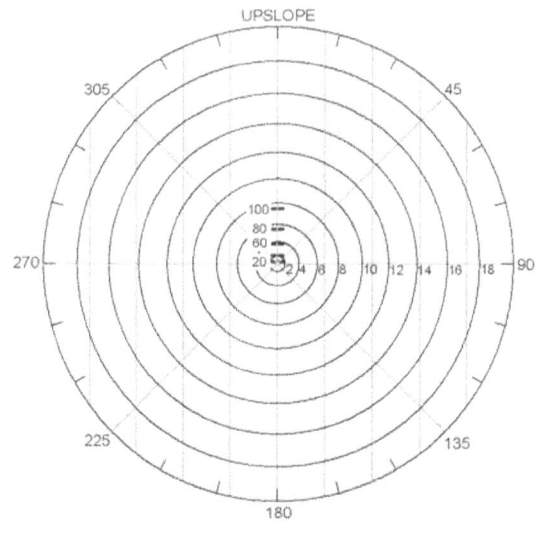

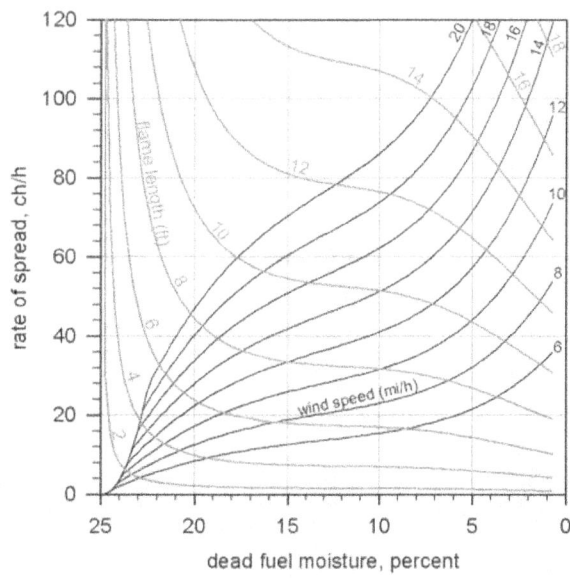

USDA Forest Service Gen. Tech. Rep. RMRS-GTR-192. 2007

117

SB3 (203)

low wind speeds

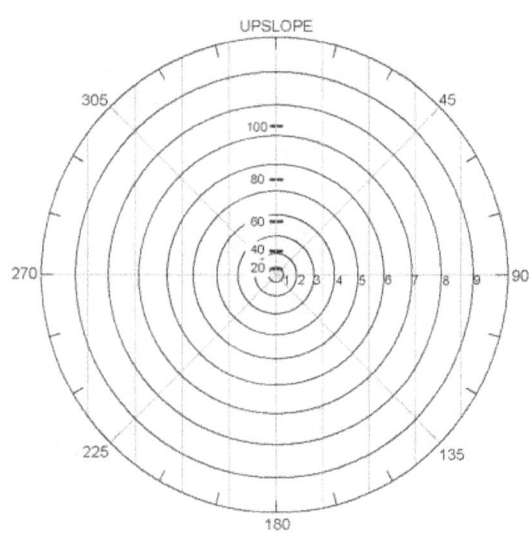

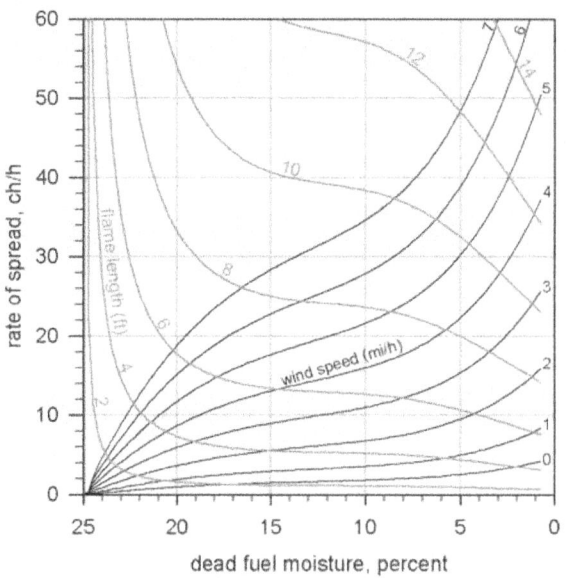

high wind speeds

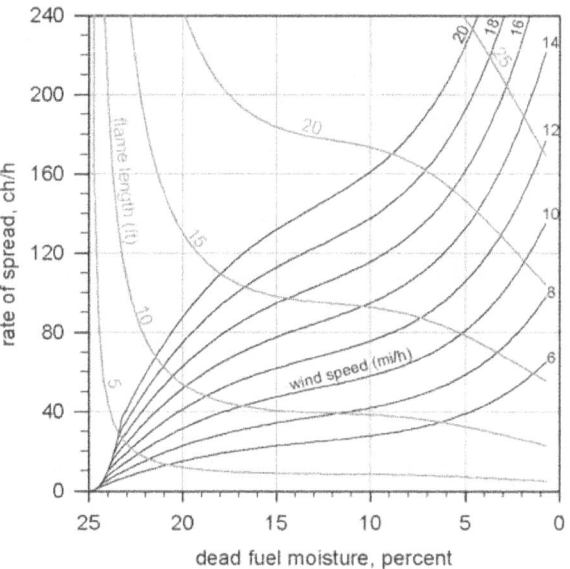

USDA Forest Service Gen. Tech. Rep. RMRS-GTR-192. 2007

SB4 (204)

low wind speeds

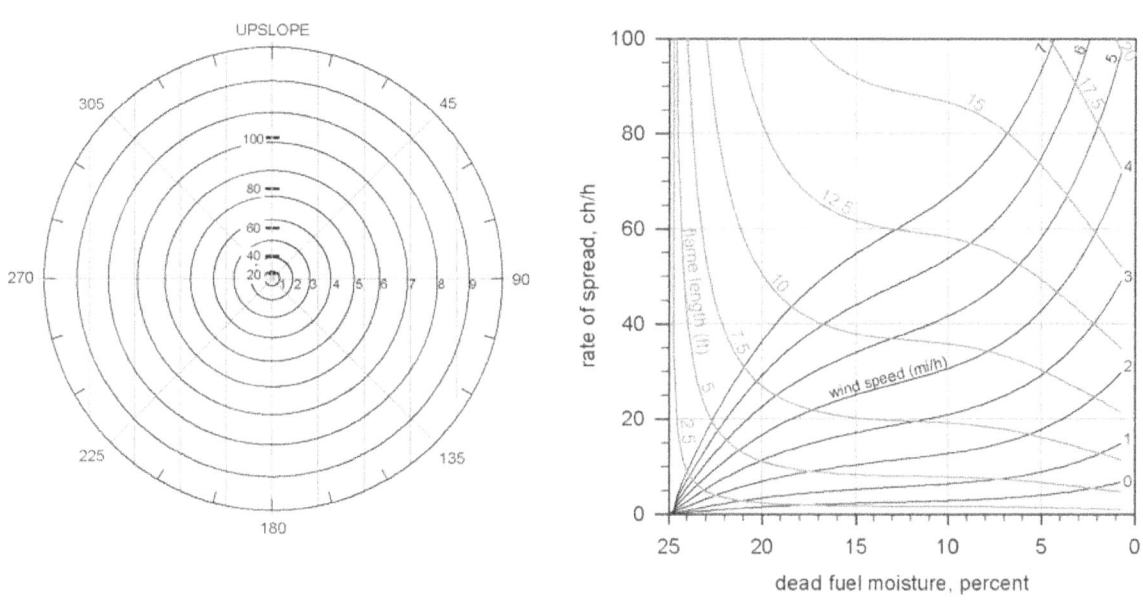

high wind speeds

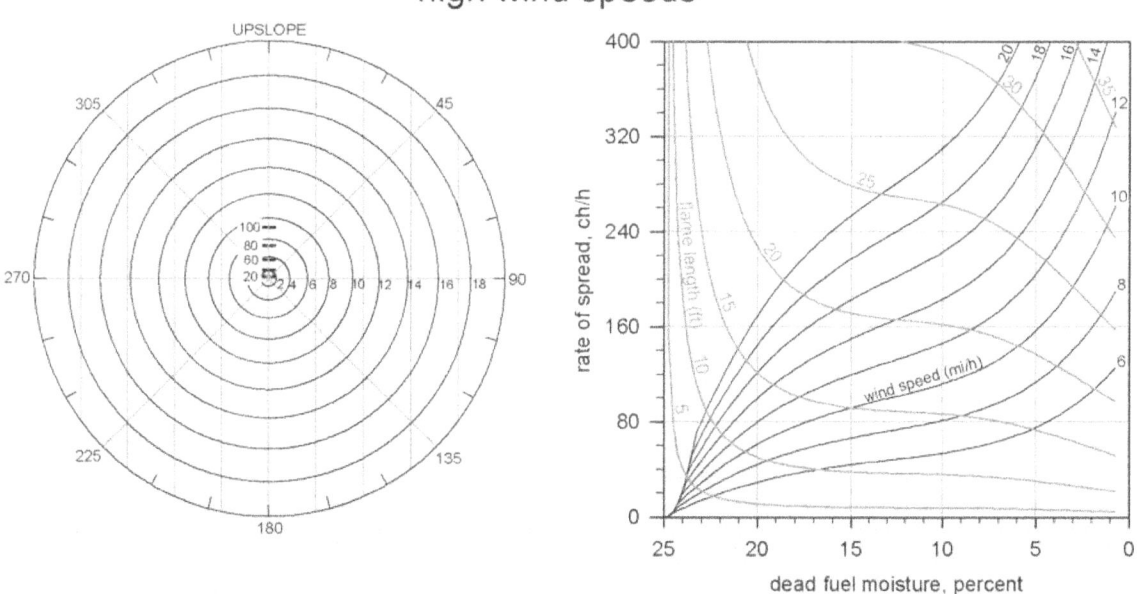

USDA Forest Service Gen. Tech. Rep. RMRS-GTR-192. 2007

119

Notes